belonging
here

belonging
here

A Guide for the Spiritually Sensitive Person

Judith Blackstone, PhD

sounds true
BOULDER, COLORADO

Sounds True, Inc.
Boulder, CO 80306

Published 2012, 2024

Jacket and book design by Dean Olson
Cover photo © Shutterstock

Printed in the United States of America

BK06803

ISBN: 9781649632005

The Library of Congress has cataloged the hardcover edition as follows:
Blackstone, Judith, 1947-Belonging here: a guide for the spiritually
sensitive person / Judith Blackstone.
  pages cm
ISBN 978-1-60407-796-4
1. Self-actualization (Psychology) I. Title.
BF637.S4B558 2012
204'.4--dc23
                                    2011049437
eBook ISBN: 978-1-60407-828-2

Contents

Introduction

Spiritual Sensitivity

ALTHOUGH WE ARE all capable of spiritual awakening, people who are drawn to the spiritual path often possess, from their earliest years, a particular kind of openness or sensitivity. This may take the form of heightened perception, abundant energy, exceptional emotional depth, or the ability to see into the truth of situations. Each of these gifts can be an entranceway into the subtle, spiritual dimension of life. They can mature into the unconditional love and clarity of spiritual realization. But when they appear in childhood, they may also produce difficulties such as conflicts in our relationships, a low tolerance for sensory stimuli, or a feeling of being at odds with the values held by our surrounding culture.

The various challenges that spiritual sensitivity may produce, and the protective strategies that we use to cope with them, can interfere with our development, and remain with us as adults. They can become obstacles in our personal and spiritual lives. They may cause us to feel alienated from the world around us and also from ourselves. Even people who have followed a spiritual path for many years may find themselves unable to proceed past a certain point in their spiritual awakening because of the impact of these early problems.

All children must find ways to cope with the challenges of their environment, the limitations or lapses in love and security that are present even in the most loving, secure families. But spiritually sensitive children face a unique set of challenges. From early on, they live in a dimension of perception, emotional experience, and insight that is not shared by most of the people around them.

Sometimes, they even look different than other people. Their bodies often seem softer or more permeable than other people's bodies. Their eyes have depth and luminosity. Their faces and bodies are often fluid and expressive, and their emotions can rock the room with their intensity. They may appear to be "deep," as if they were looking out at the world from a deeper place inside of themselves.

Especially in childhood, their softness may cause them to feel weaker than their peers. They may become the targets of bullies or relegated to the outcasts on the fringe of their school society. They may grow up feeling extremely self-conscious about their differences from other people. For example, I work with a young man who always contracts his body inward, as if to hide from sight. He feels unable to stand up to the judgment of other people, and yet, deep down, he knows that he is gifted, in a way that is difficult for him to describe to other people.

People who are spiritually open are deeply impacted by the world around them. They are usually highly empathic, experiencing the emotional and even physical suffering of others as if it were their own. They may be so aware of the suffering in the world, that it feels selfish to them to pursue their own happiness.

Another manifestation of spiritual sensitivity is an abundance of energy. All healthy children have a lit up, animated quality, but spiritually gifted children often stand out as remarkably radiant and strong-willed. This can also make them more difficult to manage, more demanding, and less compliant than their siblings.

People with abundant energy may experience themselves as larger or more powerful than others. As children, they may even feel more powerful than the adults in their lives. Some people with this sense of extraordinary power grow up afraid to experience or express the fullness of their being, for fear of alienating or injuring other people. By adulthood, they may appear particularly timid or apologetic, as a way of masking their vitality. They often express the concern that they are "too much" for other people.

Energy can be experienced as vitality, and it can also be experienced as fluidity. When people feel internally fluid, rather than feeling powerful, they may experience themselves as extremely malleable and impressionable. Instead of feeling like enclosed, separate entities, they feel permeable, like everything around them can come into them, and as if they can "leak out" into the life around them. They may feel that they merge with or even become the identities of other people they encounter. "I'm like a chameleon," a woman told me. "I become my surroundings." Although there is sometimes pleasure in the experience of becoming, or merging with other people and things, there is also confusion and exhaustion, a loss of our own moorings, as if we were "blown about by the wind."

People who are very fluid can also become easily ungrounded or diffuse. As children they may use their abundant energy to rise up above their bodies or expand outward from their bodies in order to lessen the impact of painful or overwhelming circumstances. As adults, this chronic ungrounded condition may cause them anxiety and disorientation. They feel that they have no foundation for their abundant energy, and no sense of connection to the earth. I worked with a woman who could barely feel her feet on the ground; she felt most alive in her head, or even above her head. She often complained of a lack of support from family and colleagues, and of having to make everything happen herself. This complaint stopped when she felt the support of the ground beneath her feet. She said that everything she did seemed to require less effort when she could feel herself resting on the ground.

The depth and openness of spiritually sensitive children means that they can be easily and deeply wounded, for example, by a parent's fleeting expression of anger, disappointment, or disengagement. As one woman said of her relationship with her parents, "I could feel every shift, every nuance of their emotional states." These children may be intensely affected by events that have much less impact on their siblings. As a result, they may become the "identified patient," their pain or outrage a source of bewilderment or ridicule from other family members.

Spiritually sensitive children can also suppress their experience or their self-expression with particular depth and force of will. In order to defend themselves against emotional pain, or to mold themselves to fit in with their family and peers, they may create deep fragmentations and constrictions in their bodies. As a result, there is often a striking degree of imbalance in their personal development: as adults, they present an unusual mixture of maturity and immaturity, openness and rigidity. A person may be extremely compassionate and capable of deep emotional contact with other people, and at the same time, be so severely constricted in their pelvis that they avoid intimate relationships. Or someone may exude exceptional wisdom and kindness, and yet feel so constricted in their voice that they cannot express their own needs or insights.

Children sometimes express their spiritual sensibility directly, describing experiences such as visions of subtle light, out-of-body flights, and other phenomena. If their reports of the spiritual realm are met with disbelief or censure from other family members, they will sometimes search for a context for their experiences. I know a man who, as a young child, always saw light around people. Although his parents dismissed his claims, he noticed that this light resembled the angels' haloes that were painted on the walls of their church. He kept this association to himself, but he was intrigued by this resemblance of ordinary people to angels, and comforted by the knowledge that what he could see had already been seen and recorded by other people. This explanation served him well. It allowed him to maintain and develop his subtle vision, which contributed to his exceptional ability as a healer when he grew up.

Other children may come to conclusions about their perceptions and experiences that are not so benign and that may develop into fantastical belief systems limiting their participation in life as adults. I knew a woman who, since childhood, had been able to predict events, such as the deaths of relatives, or the gender of unborn family members. She grew up believing that she had "supernatural powers" that marked her as entirely different from other human beings. Combined with her alienation from her family and her childhood religious education, this belief was a source of terror that she would suffer as terrible a death as Christ if her powers were ever exposed. It took her many years as an adult to discover that there were other people with similar gifts and that her abilities could be a source of appreciation instead of persecution.

Spiritually gifted children, because of their sensitivity, emotional responsiveness, and insight into other family members' pain, sometimes feel and appear more mature than the people around them. They seem like "old souls," alert to the suffering, hypocrisies, and complexities of family life.

This quality often casts them in the role of confidant or even of savior within the family, the one who listens to everyone's problems. They may feel that they are the only one in their family who knows what is really going on beneath the veneer of normalcy and propriety. But if they have no support for their observations, they can begin to doubt their own senses, or even their sanity. They may feel guilty about their perceptions. Or they may feel guilty for failing to heal the distress that they see in their parents and siblings.

Children who feel in some way older than their parents or teachers may grow up believing that there is no one who can actually guide or nurture them. Thus, they often lack a feeling of safety in the world. Although they may express a strong sense of independence, they also harbor a deep need to find someone who will finally take care of them. They may have a sense of having never been a child, and at the same time, of never really growing up.

They may also feel that no one can truly connect with them in the depth of their being, or truly recognize them. Or that they need to get far away from other people in order to truly be themselves. The lack of genuine connection with significant others in their childhood may derail the development of their own connection with themselves, and their ability to feel close with other people.

Spiritually sensitive people often have difficulty finding effective psychotherapy. Although they suffer from the same psychological ailments and employ many of the same defensive strategies as other people, the causes of these problems, and thus the path to resolving them, may be different for people who are spiritually open. Also, the extreme vulnerability of spiritually sensitive individuals to environmental stimuli, the intensity of their emotional pain, or their rejection of conventional social values may seem severely pathological to psychotherapists who do not have this type of sensitivity themselves. This means that their gifts may be treated as symptoms of their suffering, rather than as causes, and those aspects of themselves that they know are valuable may not be validated or developed in the therapy.

I have worked with spiritually gifted people as a psychotherapist and spiritual teacher for thirty years. Almost all of these individuals have felt some sense of being out of sync with the ordinary world, some sense of not truly belonging here. Their dilemmas—of being too impinged upon by sensory stimuli, of feeling unbearable empathy for the suffering of other people, of having no filter against the hypocrisy and brutality of the world around them, of not being able to truly connect with others or to find their true place in life—are the reasons that I have written this book. The following chapters offer a way to feel more at home in oneself and one's environment, and at the same time, to develop the gifts of sensitivity, emotional depth, and insight. They show how these gifts can be entranceways into both the everyday world of shared human connection and the most subtle, spiritual dimension of our being.

The book is divided into two parts. Part one presents the Realization Process. This is an embodied approach to spiritual awakening that includes psychological and relational healing. The first chapter in this section focuses on embodiment and its effect on our sense of identity, our experience of balance and grounding, our breath and energy, and our relationships with other people.

When we live within the internal space of the body, we feel internally whole, and at the same time, we are able to deeply and authentically connect with the world around us. By inhabiting the body, we uncover a fundamental dimension of ourselves—which I call *fundamental consciousness*—that pervades our body and environment as a unity. Because we experience this subtle consciousness pervading our body, it is the basis of direct contact with ourselves and feeling comfortable and alive within our own body. Because we experience it pervading our body and environment at the same time, it is the basis of a sense of oneness with everything and everyone that we encounter.

The relationship between mind and body, or consciousness and matter, has been a central mystery of human life throughout our history, and is still the "hard problem" for today's scientists and philosophers. Many religious traditions either ignore the body, or negate it as something to be left behind in pursuit of loftier realms, while most medical treatments ignore the influence of the mind on the body. Even if we recognize the role of the mind in illness and healing, we often speak of this in a divisive way as "mind over matter."

But even if we cannot grasp the relationship between body and mind intellectually or scientifically, we can resolve the body-mind division experientially. To inhabit our body is to become conscious throughout the whole internal space of our body. We experience that we are made of the transparency and luminosity of consciousness. At the same time, we experience that everything around us is also made of this same transparency. In this way, body-mind integration reveals the spiritual essence of our individual being and of all life.

Chapter 2 presents the main Realization Process practices. The exercises described in this chapter and throughout the book provide a way to uncover fundamental consciousness by inhabiting the internal space of the body.

These practices provide a way for us to tolerate extreme sensory sensitivity by developing our inward contact with ourselves. When we embody fundamental consciousness, the stimulation of our environment moves through our body without overwhelming us. At the same time, attunement to this dimension of ourselves can refine our perceptual ability, so that we become even more sensitive to subtle phenomena such as the vibrations of light and sound emitted by living organisms. The Realization Process exercises can also help us live comfortably with our emotional responsiveness by finding the stillness and steadiness of fundamental consciousness within the movement of our emotions. They can help us become more grounded, centered, and able to live in the world of suffering and confusion without losing connection to our own sense of truth.

Chapter 3 shows how the Realization Process exercises can help us recover from the traumatic events of our childhood. This includes ways of recognizing and releasing the protective patterns in the body that produce a sense of estrangement from ourselves and our surroundings, and that obstruct spiritual awakening.

Today we know that trauma is not limited to relatively rare events of extreme horror, such as rape, or war, or a terrible accident. Contemporary psychologists speak of "relational trauma." This is the result of painful interactions, especially in one's childhood, that are too overwhelming to be fully experienced in the moment. These "unlived" moments of fear, anger, grief, and confusion become bound up in our bodies, along with all of the various bodily attitudes that occur during these overwhelming encounters, such as cringing away from danger or deflating the chest to suppress sadness.

These events of relational trauma, especially when repeated over time, become hardened in the tissues of the body, constricting and fragmenting our body and mind so that we cannot experience ourselves as a whole within our bodies. Even though they affect the body's physical anatomy, they actually occur in a more subtle aspect of our being, in which the body and the mind are in close relationship. In order to contact and release the traumatic memories bound within our body, we have to contact ourselves inwardly. We need to find that aspect of our consciousness that is not just in our heads, but everywhere within our bodies.

Awakening to fundamental consciousness by inhabiting the body assures that we will become more alive and whole as unique human beings, at the same time as we transcend our individual selves. In this way, embodiment contributes to both psychological and spiritual maturity.

Part two of the book looks at five specific difficulties that spiritually sensitive people often face. These are the challenges of becoming resilient to sensory stimuli, being grounded and authentic, feeling content with life without losing one's compassion for the suffering around us, and accepting oneself and the world as it is. In these five chapters, by presenting some of my clients' experiences with the Realization Process exercises, I show how cultivating embodiment can help us bridge to our environment, and at the same time, progress in our openness to the spiritual dimension.

Of course, people never fit neatly into categories. Although I present stories of people who have grappled with these issues, I have taken just one thread from their complex lives to illustrate each chapter's theme. I have also combined and altered peoples' histories in order to protect their privacy. As you read this book, you may find your own unique mix of personal challenges and spiritual gifts among these categories.

I play the roles of therapist and teacher with the people who come to work with me, but I also recognize these people as my peers, my precious companions on the spiritual path. It is often said that the skillful psychotherapist or spiritual teacher serves as a kind of mirror for the client or student, in which they can see themselves with acceptance and compassion. But in my work with these spiritually gifted people, they have also been a mirror for me. They have helped me to have compassion for my own struggle to become a grounded, resilient, authentic human being and to live comfortably in a world that once seemed alien to me.

I grew up in a strictly atheist home. Yet, from earliest childhood, I sensed a kind of presence that seemed to animate the tree branches outside my bedroom window and the sky beyond them, and that was even just barely detectable in the cleanly rational air of my childhood home. I never lost my need to know this tantalizingly subtle presence, to bring it closer to myself, but for a long time, I felt that I had to keep this strange need private. I was in my late twenties before I finally discovered that there were many other people who were also following the thread of some subtle sense or intuition toward some barely tangible potential. We met in the ashrams and the newly minted Buddhist monasteries, the mystical churches and synagogues, or just "on foot," finding the way ourselves.

Zen Buddhism says of enlightened masters, "Like two thieves in the night, they recognize each other at once." But all of us on the spiritual path seem to recognize each other, and to meet each other with some relief. I hope that as you read this book you will recognize something of yourself in the following stories of healing and feel inspired and supported in developing your own spiritual gifts.

Judith Blackstone
Woodstock, New York

PART ONE

The
Realization
Process

Chapter 1

Embodiment

In the eye it sees, in the ear it hears, in the nose it smells,
in the mouth it talks, in the hand it seizes, in the leg it runs.
The source is just one illuminating essence.

RINZAI

THIS BOOK PRESENTS a method of embodied spiritual awakening called the Realization Process. By spiritual awakening, I mean a deepened and refined contact with ourselves and our surroundings that uncovers a primary essence of our being. And by embodiment, I mean an ongoing experience of living within the internal space of our body.

Living within the body and realizing this spiritual essence can help us resolve all of the challenges of spiritual sensitivity. We are able to receive the full impact of life, and even to open more fully to life, without being overwhelmed.

We become resilient to sensory stimuli and emotional suffering, we become authentic, grounded human beings, and we become more accepting of our limitations and of the pain and confusion in the world around us.

Fundamental Consciousness

The foundational essence of our being has many names in the spiritual literature of the world. It has been called Buddha-nature, wisdom mind, Self, pure consciousness, and unity consciousness, to name just a few. In the Realization Process, we call it *fundamental consciousness.*

Fundamental consciousness is experienced as a vast, unbroken stillness and spaciousness, pervading our whole body and environment as a unity. It is a profound openness to life, a direct, intimate contact with everything that we encounter.

This essence of ourselves is always there. We do not have to create it or imagine it. Because it is not something separate from ourselves, we do not know it as an object. Rather, fundamental consciousness experiences itself. It knows itself. We can say that as fundamental consciousness, we know ourselves as fundamental consciousness. We realize our basic nature.

Because this subtle consciousness pervades our body, it is the basis of our individual wholeness, our authentic sense of self. Pervading our body and environment at the same time, it is the foundation of our oneness with everything around us.

We do not lose contact with ourselves in this self-other unity, because fundamental consciousness is experienced as the ground of our individual being. As we live within the inner depths of our body and know ourselves as this essence, we experience an internal cohesion, a felt sense of our individual existence at the same time as we experience oneness with our environment. This is an interesting paradox of spiritual maturity. We become more present, unified, and complete as individuals, yet at the same time we transcend our individuality.

When I first experienced this, I was living in a Zen monastery in upstate New York. Although I loved the rituals and the rigorous meditation schedule at the monastery, I found communal life difficult. We had to eat all of our meals together, practice together, and work together, cleaning the monastery and tending to the grounds. All my life, I had found that the presence of other people disrupted my inner contact with myself—my ability to hear my own thoughts or know my own feelings. When I related with others, I usually felt merged with them. I seemed to have no barrier, no cushion between myself and the world around me, and I often had the sense of actually being pulled out of myself into my surroundings. My first months at the monastery, I felt disoriented and overwhelmed by the constant company of so many other people.

One week a month, we had *sesshin,* an intensive period of meditation practice in which we had to be completely silent, continuing our meditation even between the practice periods. This proved to be as challenging for me as "making conversation" the rest of the month. I found it almost impossible to stay calm and focused within myself with other people around me.

As the months went on, and we continued to meditate together daily, I noticed a remarkable change in my connection to both myself and the community. I seemed to be getting closer to the actual core of my body, living in a more central place in myself. As that happened, people seemed both further away from me and more accessible. I had the sense that I was relating with people across the distance between us, and yet I felt a deep kinship with them, a kind of resonance between my own being and theirs.

That summer, when I had been at the monastery for about a year, I spent many afternoons at a nearby creek. One day, I noticed that the rocks seemed strangely weightless, as if they were made of empty space. Everything I looked at had this same luminous transparency. I felt that I could easily lift the trees out of the ground or toss the boulders over my shoulder. Sitting on a bench outside the monastery that evening, I suddenly realized that I was also transparent. Instead of feeling pulled out into the space around me, I was entirely pervaded by space. My body and everything around me was made of the same luminous space.

Since that day over thirty years ago, this experience has never left me, and I have continued to open and inhabit more of my body in order to open to this spiritual essence more fully. The process of becoming more whole within myself at the same time as I become more unified with the world around me has taught me about the integration of personal and spiritual maturity, and forms the basis of many of the Realization Process practices.

Embodiment

To inhabit our body means to enter into and live within the whole internal depth of our body. It is not just being aware of our body. It is different, for example, than a "body scan," in which we shift our awareness from one part of our body to another. It is not just to be more aware of our breath or of the physical sensations within our body. When we inhabit our body, we are present within our body. We feel that we *are* the internal space of our body.

To illustrate this, take a moment to bring your awareness to your hands. As you do this, you may feel the tension or relaxation in your hands, or the warmth that they emit. You may even feel subtle currents of energy or life force within them. This is how you may experience being aware of your hands. Now, enter into them, inhabit them. Feel that you *are* the internal space of your hands. Now, you may experience them in a different way. In a sense, they experience themselves because they are no longer objects, separate from yourself.

You may wonder where you do live, if not in your body. Most people live mostly in one part of their body, such as their head or their gut. Or they may experience themselves on the surface of their body, or even in front of or above their body. Most of us grow up experiencing ourselves on the shallow interface between our body and environment, rather than experiencing ourselves all the way through the internal depth of our body. This patterning of where we live in ourselves and how we relate to our environment forms in early childhood in relation to our parents. If our parents relate mostly from their heads, for example, we will meet them there in order to connect with them. If our parents live mostly in front of their bodies, we will mirror this pattern and leave our own bodies as well. In addition to this unconscious mirroring of other people, we also protect ourselves from painful circumstances by constricting and abandoning the internal space of our bodies. I will describe this more fully in the chapter on trauma.

To experience ourselves as fundamental consciousness pervading our body means that we become conscious throughout our whole body. This gives us a sense of internal depth. We can feel that we take up space. It provides us with a sense of self-possession and self-confidence, of truly existing as a separate individual. At the same time, inhabiting our whole body at once dissolves the barrier between ourselves and our surroundings; it reveals an actual experience of oneness, or continuity, with other people and with the world around us.

Embodiment as Emptiness

We know that the body is an intricate design of anatomical structures, made of material elements such as muscle tissue, blood, and bone. But when we live within our body, we find that the internal space of the body is made of the clear open space of fundamental consciousness. In whatever part of our body we inhabit, we are open to life. We experience that part of our body as permeable rather than solid. This means that contact with the internal space of our body is the basis of openness to our environment.

For example, if you take a moment to feel that you are living within your chest, you may feel that this present moment is occurring both outside your body and within your chest at the same time. You are also available, when you live within your chest, to respond emotionally to whatever is happening in your environment. Your emotions flow more deeply and freely.

When we inhabit our whole body all the way through, we are clear-through open to our surroundings. We are completely permeable. We experience ourselves as made of empty space. We become transparent, like an empty vessel receiving each moment exactly as it is.

When we experience our own body as transparent, we also experience our whole environment as transparent, as pervaded by empty space. Then there is no barrier, no division between the life inside of our body and the life outside of ourselves in our environment. Each present moment occurs both inside and outside of us as a unity.

As fundamental consciousness, we experience ourselves and everything around us as made of empty, radiant, unified consciousness. Everything appears to be both substantial and made of empty space at the same time. Not only is consciousness integrated with our body, so that we experience our own being as made of consciousness, but consciousness appears to be integrated with all of material reality.

Sometimes this primary dimension of ourselves, integrated with all reality, is called impersonal. I do not like to use that term. It is true that the experience of fundamental consciousness is the same for all of us; it is universal. And it is true that when we realize this dimension of ourselves, there is more spontaneity in our perceptions, thoughts, and feelings. They seem to arise "on their own," without our usual strategizing and manipulation of ourselves. This is because fundamental consciousness is a dimension of disentanglement. As this dimension, we pervade our experience but we do not obstruct it. We allow life to happen, to flow.

There is really nothing more personal than this spiritual essence, because this is who we really are. It is the core of our being. Our own mind, heart, and body are revealed to be, at root, this transparent ground of consciousness. So even though, for example, our thoughts arise spontaneously, they are not "thoughts without a thinker." They are still our thoughts. If we try to make a division between our thoughts and ourselves, or our emotions and ourselves, then we construct an artificial division in what is essentially whole.

Many spiritual practices seem to offer the possibility of rising above the discomfort we feel in ourselves and in the world. They teach that we do not really exist as individuals, so we can and should disregard our emotional pain and confusion. They teach that these feelings belong to a "small self," while our true nature is a vast emptiness that has nothing to do with our human dilemmas. I do not believe that we can alleviate our emotional pain, or reach the emptiness pointed to in these spiritual teachings, by attempting to eradicate ourselves. The emptiness referred to in the teachings is not a vacancy or hollowness. It is not an escape from ourselves; it is the laying bare of ourselves.

Embodiment as Presence

Just as fundamental consciousness can be experienced as emptiness, it can also be experienced as presence, or being. This quality of presence can be experienced both within the internal space of our body and pervading our environment at the same time. Emptiness and presence are two ways of attuning to the same, unified spiritual essence of life.

Just as we can receive life throughout the internal depth of our body, we can also radiate presence—the quality of aliveness—from within our whole body. This is not a radiating from the surface of ourselves, not an expansion of ourselves into the space around us. Rather, it is a luminosity of our whole being, a glowing from within. Fundamental consciousness is both receptive and radiant.

Identity and Embodiment

Embodiment is a shift from living on the surface of the body, or even in front of or above the body, to living in the internal space of the body. This shift changes our identity, our sense of who and what we are. Most of us think of the body as something separate from ourselves. There is a division between our body and who we think we are. As a mind cut off from a body, we know ourselves as an idea or an image rather than as an embodied experience. We identify ourselves in abstract terms, according to function, such as "I am a teacher," or value, such as "I am an honest person."

When we live in the body, we know ourselves as the emptiness and presence of fundamental consciousness. We also know ourselves as the essential qualities of human existence, qualities that we share with all human beings and with other animals as well. These are qualities that we find within the body, that are uncovered or revealed as we inhabit the internal space of the body. Most of us are familiar with the feeling of love within our chests, and the recognition of this same quality in other people. But every part of our body, and every function of our being, has a "feel" to it. Our intelligence has a quality that we can feel within our heads. Our voice, or potential to speak, has a quality that we can feel within our throats. We can feel the quality of our power, or personal strength, within our midsection, and the quality of our gender within our pelvis. We do not have to create these qualities; we discover them as part of the process of embodiment. This gives us a felt sense, a qualitative experience, of existing, rather than an abstract idea of who we are. So embodiment is a shift from an abstract or "narrative" sense of self to a qualitative experience of self.

In addition to this qualitative sense of self that is the same in everyone, embodiment also helps us know our individual selves more clearly; for example, our own aspirations, talents, needs, and preferences. The twentieth century Zen Buddhist philosopher Nishitani, describing emptiness, says: "It is the field in which each and every thing—as an absolute center, possessed of an absolutely unique individuality—becomes manifest as it is in itself."[1] The clear space of fundamental consciousness reveals us to ourselves, intimately and specifically.

Embodiment and Wholeness

When we live within the internal space of our body, we become seamless. We have a sense of internal continuity within our whole body. Even our breath moves in our whole body, not just in our lungs.

As this unified being, we can experience all of the parts and aspects of ourselves at once. We can experience the internal space of our legs and our head simultaneously, for example. We can think, feel, and sense at the same time. This means that all aspects of our self-expression contain the full breadth of our being. For example, our whole being will be reflected in the timbre of our voice, in the way that we touch or move. Our reception of life also becomes whole. The Zen philosopher Dogen called this "seeing and hearing with the whole body and mind." I will say more about the wholeness of the senses in the next chapter.

The Whole Body Breath

Embodiment transforms the breath. As we live within our whole body, we can experience our whole body breathing at once. Instead of feeling that the breath just goes into our chest or our belly, we can feel the vibration of breath in every part of our body simultaneously. This is because as we inhabit our body, our breath becomes increasingly refined and integrated with our energy system, which is everywhere in our body.

When we live within our body, our breath becomes lighter and quieter. Usually, our breath is limited by muscular tensions. It may skip and jolt, as if it were running over bumpy roads. But in the body of fundamental consciousness, the breath is smooth and continuous.

The breath carries the emotions that we hold in our bodies. If we have sadness in our body, for example, the breath will feel and even sound sad, as if we were sighing. If we have anger bound in our body, our breath will carry anger's fiery hiss. If we have fear in our body, our breath will sound fearful, as if we were gasping.

The breath also reflects the imbalance in the body. When we live more in the top of our body, for example, we bring our breath in through the tops of our nostrils. The pathway of the breath angles upward and continues to stimulate those parts of ourselves where we are already overstimulated. When we live more in the bottom of the body, we bring our breath in through the bottom of our nostrils (closest to our upper lip). As we inhabit our whole body, the breath comes in through the centers of the nostrils and reaches everywhere in our body at once.

Balance and Grounding

As you will see in the next chapter, one of the ways that we enter into fundamental consciousness in the Realization Process is by balancing our awareness within our body; for example, we find the inside of our shoulder sockets, and then balance our awareness of these two points. It requires a very subtle, very fine level of awareness in order to find both these points at the same time, rather than moving our focus back and forth between them.

The physicist Heinz Pagels once wrote that material existence is the product of a broken symmetry.[2] Everything in life moves because of life's imbalance. Since fundamental consciousness is experienced as absolutely still and unchanging, we can say that it is the dimension of perfect balance. Perhaps it is because of this still point, this balanced dimension at the core of our being, that human beings possess an innate sense of balance. We recognize balance, or harmony, in all aspects of our lives as ease and beauty.

Since balance is an attribute of fundamental consciousness, it is synonymous with openness and self-contact. The more inward contact we achieve, the more we experience balance, or symmetry, throughout the internal space of our body. This means, for example, that we can experience the internal space of both of our arms at the same time, or the internal space of both of our shoulder or hip sockets at the same time.

The embodiment of this balanced dimension can also be understood as our relationship with gravity, or with the ground beneath us. Usually we think of the body as a solid mass, and gravity as working against that mass, trying to tip it over. We think that we need to exert muscular strength in order to withstand gravity's tipping influence. But the physical body is not solid. We can experience ourselves as made of the clear empty space of consciousness. The more open we become, the more symmetrical our internal experience of ourselves becomes and the more evenly we settle the internal space of our body toward the ground. This is another way of saying that to become open is to let go of our protective grip on ourselves; for example, if we have been constricting our chest against feeling emotional pain, and we let go of this constriction, the internal space of our chest will become more symmetrical and will relax and settle toward the ground in a more even way. As we inhabit our whole body, every part of our body begins to relax and settle toward the ground in this way.

The more evenly we settle toward the ground, the more we can experience an upward current of energy that rises from the ground and moves through the internal space of our body, making it light and buoyant, supporting our ability to sit upright or to stand. In this way, gravity works not on the body, but through it. As we become more open and balanced, we settle on the earth with our whole being.

This aspect of embodiment, our increasing sense of being supported by the ground, goes a long way toward alleviating

the sense of not belonging here that so many spiritually sensitive people feel. Yet this initial letting down, or giving in, to
the pull of the earth, is often resisted by spiritually sensitive
individuals. Recently a woman told me that she felt "resent-
ment" when I asked her to settle in this way. She enjoyed a
sense of floating upward with her head and chest. When she
relaxed in her body, she felt earthbound in a way that did not
feel spiritual to her. However, after some practice, she was
able to feel the upward current coming up from the ground
so that she had a sense of floating with her whole body, not
just with her head and chest, at the same time as she felt connected with the earth. This shift is important not just for our
personal comfort but also for our spiritual maturity. If we
open just the top of our body, we do not arrive at the most
subtle spiritual dimension of our being because fundamental
consciousness is a dimension of wholeness and requires that
we open to it with our whole body.

When I was a young woman, I was a professional dancer,
until a severe back injury ended my career. The injury was
augmented by surgery that fused my spine in the unbal-
anced, injured position. Unable to dance and uncomfortable
in any position, I would often lie on the floor of my dance
studio and pray for healing. One day, I noticed that as I
surrendered my weight to the ground, there was a spontaneous movement deep within my body toward balance. The
more I relaxed, the more distinct this movement became. I
also found that I could increase this spontaneous movement
within my body if I balanced my awareness; for example, if

I found a point to the right and the left of my head at the same time, my body would drop more completely toward the ground and would move toward alignment without any effort on my part. Finally, I could feel currents of energy rising from the ground and pulling the internal space of my body toward symmetry.

Later, living at the Zen monastery, I felt this same spontaneous movement during sitting meditation. The downward pull of gravity and the upward current of energy rising from the ground actually move us toward balance if we do not impede their action. When we meditate, we are opening to this natural movement. By sitting still and relaxing our grip on ourselves, we are allowing gravity to draw us toward balance, and thus toward openness, and the spiritual dimension.

Fluidity

When we know ourselves as fundamental consciousness, all of our responses flow through this ground of our being without getting stuck anywhere. This is absolute receptivity. All of our ideas, all of our fixed attitudes and protective strategies, give way to the reception of experience. We can feel an emotion deep within our heart, for example, but we will not hold on to it; the emotion will move through us. Thoughts will flow through our mind, but they will not become obsessive "tape loops." We can also allow the vibrations of other human beings to flow through this fundamental dimension of ourselves, without being overwhelmed by them.

This means that we no longer get in the way of our own responses, our creativity, our pleasure. In this way, embodiment is the basis of spontaneity and freedom. It is an experience of both all-pervasive stillness and fluidity (the flow of life) at the same time. Even our own thoughts can surprise us; even familiar sights and sounds register with the impact of newness.

Movement

Embodying ourselves as fundamental consciousness also allows our movement to become more fluid. When people experience themselves only as physical matter, they move only their physical body. In other words, they experience themselves as moving just the muscular surface of themselves; they feel as if their body is composed of big solid chunks of matter that can only be moved at the joints in the skeleton.

But as the internal space of our body becomes more unified, there are fewer gaps in our contact with ourselves, and there are fewer gaps in our movement: if we lift an arm, the movement flows through the whole internal continuity of our arm, from the shoulder socket to the tips of our fingers. It feels as if every cell is involved in the movement. This brings breadth, or qualitative richness, to our movements or gestures.

Interestingly, although the English language recognizes the richness of vocal resonance or timbre, we do not have words to describe this same phenomenon in movement. Spiritually embodied movement has been noted in many

Zen Buddhist stories, however. In one story, the Zen master Joshu goes to visit two hermits who are practicing in their mountain retreats. At the first hut, Joshu calls out, "Anybody in, anybody in?" The hermit thrusts up his fist. Joshu remarks, "The water is too shallow for a ship to anchor." At the second hut, he calls out again, "Anybody in, anybody in? The second hermit also thrusts up his fist. Joshu bows to him.[3] The Zen master can see, in each hermit's gesture, the depth of his practice. The second hermit is present in his arm. His body and his mind have become one.

Matter, Energy, and Fundamental Consciousness

We can divide our organism into three levels: matter, energy, and fundamental consciousness. These are three levels of attunement to ourselves. As we reach the most subtle attunement—to fundamental consciousness—we do not lose our experience of ourselves as energy or matter. Rather, we have a sense of pervading and encompassing the material and energetic components of our being.

Most people never get to know themselves beyond the level of physical matter. They experience themselves as solid objects, and they experience other people, animals, trees, and so forth as solid objects also. In their relationships, they make contact from the surface of themselves to the surface of others, because a solid object has only a surface. In their relationship with their body, they are generally concerned with remaining as "solid" as possible. Our cultural ideal (and our cultural ignorance) is summed up in the term "hardbody." We associate firmness and solidity with strength and youthfulness.

Martial arts masters have shown us that when energy (which they call *qi* or *chi*) is combined with physical movement, our strength is increased. Energy pervades the whole body. Tai chi masters speak of the most advanced phase of their practice as attunement to energy even within the marrow of the bones. In the past thirty years or so, psychotherapy and bodywork techniques that work on the energy system have become quite well-known. From these therapies we have learned that emotional trauma, physical injury, and illness are all associated with constrictions in our energy system. When energy circulates freely in the body, we feel more emotional capacity, more comfortable in our body, and we enjoy greater health and vitality. So the sense of youthfulness and even the maintenance of a vibrant, youthful appearance depend on the circulation of energy in the body.

Information about energy, in the body and in the universe, is now easily available. But fundamental consciousness, the innermost dimension of ourselves, is less well-known. Very few psychological or bodywork techniques address this level. Even in Buddhist and Hindu practices, to realize this most subtle dimension is considered to be the most advanced phase of spiritual realization, and is not widely taught. But I have found that many people today have the sensitivity to attune to and live in this most subtle ground of their being.

Fundamental consciousness is a dimension of stillness and silence. When we know ourselves as this primary stillness, our energy can move more freely and deeply through us, without overwhelming or in any way altering our basic identity. As this stillness, we also reach a more subtle level of our energy dimension. We can see, hear, and feel a fine vibration, pervading our body and environment.

This primary dimension of consciousness is often described, in both the Buddhist and Hindu teachings, as "distributed awareness," possessing neither boundaries nor center. What is not often taught is that we cannot uncover this unbounded expanse of consciousness unless we let go of ourselves from deep within our whole body. This subtle consciousness pervades both our own form and everything around us equally. We need to be present within our own form in order to open to the transparency of our most subtle dimension of consciousness.

A woman came to work with me who had been engaged in Buddhist practice for several decades. She felt that there must be some basic deficit in herself that she was still not able to experience the luminous emptiness that her teachers had promised. When I watched her meditate, I saw that her focus was on the space outside of and around her head. She also relaxed into a diffuse, dreamy state. When I guided her through the Realization Process exercise of inhabiting her body, she at first felt resistance to experiencing inward contact with herself. She said, "I thought I was supposed to be non-local," and she gestured outward to the room.

But as she began to inhabit her body, she noticed that many of the obstacles that she had struggled with in her years of spiritual practice dissolved. She said that she could finally experience what the Buddhist teachings meant by direct experience. She said, "When I am in my body, I no longer have ideas about myself. I just am."

Fundamental consciousness is not something we create; rather, it is self-arising. It appears spontaneously as we become more open throughout our whole body. If we just attempt to be non-local, then we create a schism in ourselves that takes us further away from spiritual awakening. When the woman I just described was able to inhabit her body, her meditation lost its diffuse, dreamy quality. She found herself in (and as) the crisp, radiant expanse of sheer transparency, pervading both her internal and external experience as a whole.

The Body and Religion

Many spiritual teachings, including Eastern teachings, negate the body as something less than spiritual. In our own culture there is an old belief that God does not love the body. Even though I was brought up in a family that disdained religion, I have imprinted in my mind the storybook image of a contrite and unhappy Adam and Eve, their eyes downcast toward the leaves that cover their genitals. The many sophisticated interpretations of this story that I have read since childhood have not erased the more primal message that God's anger had something to do with Adam and Eve's naked bodies and unstoppable appetites. Even if we are a long way from believing this story, its legacy still haunts our culture and has some effect on all of us.

These archaic religious images teach that the body is the cause of human misbehavior and suffering, as if it could act on its own depraved impulses apart from the noble intentions of the heart and mind. Even though the media bombards us with sensual displays, the very brashness and superficiality of these images supports the notion that we can only have the pleasures of the body if we sacrifice the rewards of the spirit. This belief system also teaches that the truly advanced souls, the saints and holy men of Western religion, all managed a total disregard for the body in order to be closer to God.

Related to the belief that God does not love the body is the cultural belief that we cannot truly love each other's bodies, that there are only specific types of bodies, very rare types, that can be loved. For the sake of love, the body is starved, drugged, and overexercised. It is finally a phantom body that we send out to search for love—a body devoid of character or age, so distorted that it is hardly capable of human contact.

Underlying these beliefs is the idea that the body is something separate from the person—that it is possible to have sexual pleasure without involving the spirit, or that it is possible to have spiritual fulfillment without a body. But neither can we have our whole individual being nor our spiritual oneness with the world around us unless we include the body in our realization, unless we experience that even our body is made of fundamental consciousness. To realize fundamental consciousness is to know and live in our body, all the way through to its primary dimension. This means that spiritual essence is grounded in the body, and that even the ordinary movements of daily life can sustain and deepen our spiritual realization.

The spiritual essence of ourselves is our actual nature, always present beneath the polished surface of our lives, more durable than all of our protective posturing. It shines through the cracks in our defenses, and thrives on our crumbling facades. Once uncovered, it pervades and radiates throughout our body and everything around us—no matter what we are doing or feeling. This unfettered being does not resemble the fearful vision of untamed desire run amok. Rather, our true, wild nature is the fundamental unity of our mind, heart, and body.

Sometimes people ask me, "What is the point of spiritual realization? Will it make me more efficient at my job, richer, will it help me find a relationship?" The depth of contact with ourselves that we gain in embodied spiritual awakening helps every aspect of our functioning, including our ability to concentrate, to create favorable circumstances in our lives, to feel less lonely, and to choose more satisfying relationships. These things are really secondary to the experience of spiritual realization itself. It is like saying that we should have sex because we will feel more relaxed afterwards. Although this is true, the resulting relaxation is not nearly as compelling as the sensations and feelings of the experience of sex itself, or the satisfaction of fulfilling an innate hunger.

Embodied spiritual realization fulfills our innate hunger for contact with ourselves. It is our most intimate knowledge of ourselves and our world, and the source of our most

profound pleasure. It is the wide-awake, exquisite sensitivity
of all our senses, and the basis of our truest perception, feeling, knowledge, and expression.

Chapter 2

The Realization Process: Practices for Embodied Spiritual Awakening

Every being is changed to a perfectly coherent radiance made transparent through the illumination of the transcendent.

YUASA

THE REALIZATION PROCESS is a method of realizing spiritual oneness, or nonduality. However, it differs from most other methods of spiritual awakening in its focus on embodiment and relationship and in its understanding of the individual self. In this chapter, I present the main

27

Realization Process exercises, and I will describe other supplemental practices throughout the rest of the book. In part two of the book, I show, through the stories of people who have come to work with me, how these practices can be applied to some specific challenges of spiritual sensitivity. These exercises cultivate perception, emotional responsiveness, and mental clarity, while at the same time helping to develop tolerance to the sensory stimuli, emotional pain, and mental confusion in our environment.

Today, many spiritual techniques, especially of nondual awakening, work mainly with the mind. They are concerned with recognizing and cutting through the mental concepts that may limit or distort our perception of the present moment. Students of these methods are usually instructed to train their attention on whatever is happening in each moment. However, attention is volitional— it requires the activity of being attentive. But fundamental consciousness arises spontaneously; it is beyond our volition. It is simply there when we inhabit and open our body. Once we can live within our body, we do not need to hold an attitude of attention. The realization of fundamental consciousness becomes an ongoing, effortless transformation of the way we experience ourselves and our environment.

Fundamental consciousness is also more subtle than attention. Rather than focusing *on* objects, it pervades everything that it perceives. It is both subject and object at the same time.

Another popular method for realizing nonduality is to let go of any manipulation of ourselves or our environment.

This approach can help us relax and accept life as it. But when people are instructed to "just let go," they usually let go into the space around them. This is an energetic expansion outward into the environment. It will not uncover the extremely subtle dimension of transparency that pervades the body and environment as a unity. To actually realize this fundamental or nondual consciousness, we need to let go of ourselves from deep within the body. The Realization Process exercises cultivate inward contact with the body, so that we can let go into this most subtle dimension of ourselves.

It is important to understand that nondual realization is completely effortless; it arises without any contrivance or manipulation of ourselves. The Realization Process techniques are just exercises, requiring concentration and focus; they are not the realization itself. This effort of inner-focused work is a direct path to letting go from the core of our being into the effortless dimension of fundamental consciousness. After you practice each exercise, I suggest that you sit for a while and relax in the clear space that pervades your body and environment.

Attuning to Fundamental Consciousness

The first Realization Process exercise is the attunement to fundamental (nondual) consciousness. This exercise cultivates both the emptiness and the quality-rich presence of our spiritual essence. It begins with inhabiting the body, and then proceeds to attuning to the space that pervades both the body and environment as a unity. As I've said, to *inhabit* your body is different than being *aware* of your body. To inhabit your feet, for example, means that you feel present within your feet. You feel that you *are* the internal space of your feet; this is part of who you are. So this exercise is not a body scan; rather, it is a practice of entering into and living within the internal space of the body.

If you feel that you do not have much internal contact with yourself, or that you are easily displaced by the world around you, you may want to do just the beginning of the first exercise, in which you inhabit your body. As you inhabit your body, you begin to possess yourself from the inside; you reclaim the internal space of your body. You will feel that you have internal volume, that you take up space. With practice, you will begin to feel that you exist internally, that there is an actual internal substance to your being. This substance, as I have said, feels both empty and radiant at the same time. It is completely transparent, like empty space, and it is full of the essential qualities of your aliveness. Once you feel established in (or as) this internal space, you can go on to experience that this emptiness and radiant presence pervades both your body and everything around you, at the same time.

Most people are not aware of the qualities of their being. As I explained in the last chapter, all of the various parts of our body, and all of the functions of our being associated with the different parts of our body, have a quality, a "feel." These qualities are the same, or very similar, in all of us. Just as we can recognize love in another person because it is the same as our own feeling of love, all of the qualities of our being are universal. We can even observe and connect with these qualities in animals. All of nature, as it becomes more conscious, displays these innate qualities of the fundamental dimension of being. To experience these various internal qualities helps us shift from an abstract idea of ourselves to a qualitative or actual experience of ourselves. It also helps us experience our oneness with other people and with all of nature. In the relational exercises described later in this chapter, you will see that these qualities are part of our deepest, spiritual connection with other people.

Of the various qualities that we attune to in the first Realization Process exercise, the quality of gender is often the most difficult for people to feel. This is because most people live more in the top of their bodies than the bottom. The negation or suppression of sexuality, which has been passed down from one generation to the next, is a common, culture-wide holding pattern. Children are taught very early that the bottom of their body must be kept hidden, and many are even taught that the feelings associated with that part of the body are "dirty" or "bad." Even if there is more acceptance of our sexual nature now than there was in past generations, the holding pattern associated with these attitudes toward sexuality is passed down through the generations as children mirror the way their parents live in their bodies. If the parents suppress the feelings in the bottom of their bodies, their children will often unconsciously mirror that pattern. But as we inhabit the pelvis, and all of the anatomy of our gender, we will experience a quality of gender.

Some people experience their gender as different than their biological gender. This is why, in the exercise, I ask you to attune to the quality of gender, "however that feels to you." The exercise does not call for a specifically male or female quality. As long as you can attune to the quality of that part of your being, you will be able to realize the wholeness of fundamental consciousness. Sometimes people associate themselves with a different gender because they don't want to be bound by the behaviors or limitations that society has attributed to their biological gender. It is important to understand that this exercise has nothing to do with those behaviors. To experience a female quality of gender, for example, does not mean to experience yourself as "nurturing," or "intuitive." The quality of gender can be felt anywhere on the spectrum from female to male. However you experience it, it is still noticeably different than the other qualities of being, such as power or love.

The connection between the physical anatomy and the qualitative/functional aspect of being is quite simple. The more we inhabit our chest (that is, the more inward contact we have with our chest), the more deeply we feel emotion. The more fully we inhabit our sexual organs, the more intense is our sexual feeling. To inhabit the whole body at once integrates the qualities and functions of our being. If we inhabit our chest and head at the same time, we can feel and think at the same time. In this way, the exercise of inhabiting the body can help heal the fragmentation between our cognitive and emotional functions.

It is these essential aspects of our being (gender, power, love, voice, and understanding) that, when we are very young, we constrict in response to painful or confusing events and relationships. So, in order to become whole, to realize the dimension of wholeness, we need to attune to and recover these primary qualities of our being.

You will see in the first exercise that I also ask you to attune to the quality of "self" within your body. This is a particular quality that is also the same in all of us—that feels like "self." This quality has always been there, in the background of all the flow of your experience. Because it is always there, I have found that almost everyone can attune to this quality. I use the attunement to the quality of self because it is very effective at helping us enter into the subtle, unified dimension of fundamental consciousness. Even attuning to the quality of self in one part of your body, such as your feet, can help you experience your spiritual essence throughout your whole body. Words such as "being" or "essence" do not seem to evoke the primary level of being as effectively as the word "self."

Note that sometimes when I teach this exercise, I ask people to attune to the quality of "self" within the body, and other times I ask them to attune to the quality of "your self." The quality of "self" is the same quality as "your self." The quality of self that we all experience is both universal and personal at the same time. It is the same quality in all of us, but it is also the feeling of the primary dimension of our own individual self.

EXERCISE 1 Attunement to Fundamental Consciousness: Inhabiting the Body

This exercise is best practiced sitting on a chair with your back straight and your feet on the ground. (Once you become familiar with the exercise, you can practice it in any position.)

Close your eyes.

Begin by focusing on your breath. Observe how the breath comes in and out of your nose.

Silently count two counts to inhale and two counts to exhale, so that your breath becomes smooth and even.

Bring your inhale inward through your head, so that you use your inhale to make deep inward contact with yourself. Let your exhale release naturally, without directing it.

Bring your attention down to your feet. Feel that you are inside your feet, that you inhabit your feet. Let yourself feel that you *are* the internal space of your feet, that this is part of who you are.

Now attune to the quality of your self (not an idea, but a particular quality that feels like "self") inside your feet.

Make sure that you can remain in your feet as you breath—that your inhale does not lift you upward, out of your feet.

Feel that you are inside your ankles and your lower legs. Attune to the quality of your self inside your ankles and lower legs.

34

Feel that you are inside your knees. Settle down into your knees until they feel soft. Balance your awareness of the space inside your knees, finding both of those internal areas at the same time.

Experience the absolute stillness of the balanced mind. Fundamental consciousness is experienced as stillness because it is the dimension of perfect balance. So to find the space inside both knees at the same time can help you enter into, or uncover, the dimension of fundamental consciousness. You will find that very subtle attunement is required in order to find the inside of both knees at exactly the same time (without going back and forth between them).

Feel that you are inside your thighs. Attune to the quality of your self inside your thighs.

Feel, with a very subtle mind, that you are inside your hip sockets. From the inside of your hip sockets, you can feel the internal space of your upper thighs and the internal space of your lower torso at the same time.

Balance your awareness of the space inside your hip sockets, finding the inside of both hip sockets at the same time. Experience the stillness of your balanced mind and the movement of your breath at the same time. The mind is still and balanced, and the breath is moving.

This part of the exercise can help you experience that all of the content of your experience—all of your thoughts, emotions, sensations, and perceptions—moves through the stillness of fundamental consciousness, without disturbing that stillness. As fundamental consciousness, you experience both the luminous, motionless space of the ground, and the movement of life—at the same time.

Feel that you are inside your pelvis. Attune to the quality of your gender inside your pelvis (again, not an idea but a feeling, however your gender feels to you). Bring your breath down into your pelvis and let it pass through the quality of gender inside your pelvis.

Feel that you are inside your midsection, between your ribs and your pelvis, including the solar plexus area under the ribs. Attune to the quality of your power, your personal strength, inside your midsection. Bring your breath down into your midsection and let it pass through the quality of power inside your midsection.

Feel that you are inside your chest (all the way through to your back). Attune to the quality of your love inside your chest. This doesn't need to be a big feeling, just a little of the tenderness that you have inside your chest. Let your love rest in your chest. Bring your breath down into your chest and let it pass through the quality of love inside your chest.

Feel that you are inside your shoulders. Attune to the quality of your self inside your shoulders.

Feel, with a very subtle mind, that you are inside your shoulder sockets. From the inside of your shoulder sockets, you can feel the internal space of your upper arms and the internal space of your upper torso at the same time. Balance your awareness of the space inside your shoulder sockets; find the inside of both shoulder sockets at the same time. Experience the stillness of the balanced mind and the movement of your breath passing through the stillness without disturbing the stillness.

Feel that you are inside your arms, wrists, and hands, all the way to your fingertips. Attune to the quality of your self inside your arms, wrists, and hands.

Feel that you are inside your neck. Attune to the quality of your voice, your potential to speak, inside your neck. Bring your breath down into your neck and let it pass through the quality of your voice inside your neck.

Feel that you are inside your head and behind your whole forehead, all the way around to your temples. Find a point in the center of your forehead (not between the brows but in the center of your forehead). Keep that point steady as you breathe. The point may move around as you inhale and exhale. See what you need to let go of in order for the point to remain steady.

Now get back behind that point so that you are seeing it from behind, from deep inside your head. With practice, you may be able to see a point, or a sphere of light in the center of your forehead.

Feel that you are inside your eyes. Let your eyes soften so that they feel continuous with the rest of your face. Feel that you are behind your cheekbones and inside your nose, all the way to the tip of your nose. Feel that you are inside your jaw, your mouth, your lips, and your chin. Feel that you are inside your ears.

Now feel that you are inside your whole brain. Attune to the quality of your understanding inside your whole brain. Bring your breath through your head and let it pass through the quality of understanding inside your brain. See if you can feel the breath moving through both sides of your brain.

Now feel that you are inside your whole body all at once. If we say that the body is the temple, you are sitting inside the temple. Attune to the quality of your self in your whole body. Experience that you are made of the quality of self, all the way through your body. Breathe smoothly and evenly.

Keeping your eyes closed, find the space outside your body, the space in the room.

Experience that the space inside your body and the space outside your body is the same, continuous space; it pervades you. You are still inside your body, but your body is pervaded by space. You are permeable, transparent. Let your breath move through the space.

Slowly open your eyes. Again feel that you are inside your whole body at once. Attune to the quality of your self in your whole body. Find the space outside your body. Feel that the space inside and outside of your body is the same, continuous space. It pervades you.

Experience that the space pervading your body also pervades everything in your environment. You are still inside your whole body as you experience this. Do not project yourself through the things around you in the room. This is not an expansion of yourself out into space, but an attunement to the space that seems to be there already, pervading you and everything around you.

Experience that the space pervading your body also pervades the walls of the room. That's how subtle it is; it pervades even the walls, the floor and the ceiling. Remain inside your whole body while you experience the space pervading you and the walls of the room.

The Subtle Core of the Body

When we attune to ourselves as fundamental consciousness, we reach a more subtle level of our energy system. This is a very fine vibration that is felt together with the stillness of fundamental consciousness. The next exercise, the core breath, can help you cultivate this very subtle level of energy.

The core breath exercise attunes to a subtle channel that runs through the vertical core of the body, from the center of the bottom of your pelvis to the center of the top of your head. This is sometimes called the "wisdom channel" or the "central channel." In yoga, it is referred to by its Sanskrit name *shushumna nadi*. It is our entranceway into the pervasive spaciousness of fundamental consciousness. The more contact we have with this subtle channel, the more complete is our realization of fundamental consciousness. When we can let go of ourselves and our environment from the subtle core of the body, then we let go into the spaciousness of fundamental consciousness. When we can live, effortlessly, in the subtle core of the body, we have an ongoing realization of ourselves and our environment as made of fundamental consciousness.

This innermost core of the body feels like the center of our being. It feels like we are living in the center of all our experience, as a witness and completely immersed in our life at the same time. In this subtle core, we gain our deepest perspective on our environment (because we are perceiving it from the distance of this innermost core of ourselves) as we experience oneness with our environment. The subtle core of the body also integrates all of the qualities and functions of our body and being. When we live in the subtle core, we can think, feel, and sense at the same time.

We can enter into the subtle core of the body anywhere along it. In the Realization Process, we begin by entering through three main points: the center of the head, the center of the chest, and the center of the pelvis. The center of your head is between your ears, the very center of the internal space of your head. The center of your chest and pelvis are in the center of each of these areas, but back toward your spine, as deeply inward as you can focus, without strain. For those readers familiar with the chakras, the chest center is the same as the heart chakra in yoga, and the pelvis center is between the second and third chakras.

In this exercise, we find these three points along the core of the body, and we initiate our breath within these points. When we breathe within the core of our body, our breath becomes unified with our energy dimension. As this very subtle breath/energy, the whole internal space of our body breathes at once. This produces a subtle vibration throughout our whole body. One student described this subtle vibration as feeling like a "fine champagne."

This core breath exercise asks you to feel a vibration throughout the whole subtle core of your body, as you breathe within each of the points. Do not direct your breath to the whole core, but allow this vibration to occur as a result of breathing within each of the points. As you progress in your practice of this exercise, you will be able to feel this vibration not only along the core, but throughout your whole body. You may also begin to feel that there is a mental quality to the breath, as if the mind were breathing within the core points. I do not mean your thinking mind, but rather a mental quality that feels as if your mind is breathing.

EXERCISE 2 Core Breath

This exercise should be practiced sitting upright on a chair or cushion.

Close your eyes.

Find the center of your head. This point is between your ears, between your face and the back of your head, the very center of the inside of your head. Many people une to this center too high up in their heads. When contact the center of your head, you may feel an automatic connection down through the whole core of your body.

Inhaling through your nose, bring the breath into the center of your head. Exhale through your nose. The breath needs to be subtle to move through your head to the center.

Now initiate the breath from within the center of the head, so that the center of the head draws in the breath— as if you have air in the center of your head that you can breathe. The exhale is a release from within the center of the head. This is an internal breath. You are not bringing breath to the point, but rather initiating the breath from within the point. It feels as if you are inhaling and exhaling within the subtle core of the body. By breathing within the center of your head, you can feel a subtle vibration throughout the whole subtle core of your body.

From the center of your head, find your heart center, in the center of your chest but deep in the subtle core of the body. You can leave the center of your head now, and you are just in your heart center.

Now initiate your breath within your heart center. Your exhale is a release from within the heart center. Again, do not bring your breath to the heart center, but feel that the breath begins there. The first place you feel your breath move, before you feel it move in your lungs, is within the heart center. By breathing within your heart center, you can feel a vibration throughout the whole subtle core your body.

Find the center of your head again. From the center of your head, find your pelvic center, an inch or two below your navel, deep in the subtle core of the body, between the second and third chakras.

Initiate your breath within your pelvic center. Your exhale is a release from within the pelvic center. By breathing within the pelvic center, you can feel a vibration throughout the whole subtle core of your body.

Now all three centers at the same time: find the center of your head again. Find the center of your head and your heart center at the same time. Find all three centers at the same time.

Initiate the breath from within all three centers at the same time. The exhale is a release from within all three centers. Make sure that you do not leave out the center of the head; keep the center of your head breathing and add in the other two as you can. The advanced instruction is to feel that the mind is breathing within all three centers; there is a mental quality to the breath.

Open your eyes. Find the center of your head, your heart center, and your pelvic center at the same time. Let yourself experience the room from this core of yourself. Usually we experience our environment from the surface of ourselves, so it may feel like a shift to experience the room from your core. Continue to initiate the breath from within all three centers at the same time. You may be able to feel that you can let go of all of the content of experience, internal and external, on both your inhale and your exhale. Everything will still be there, but you are letting go of your grasp on it.

The Essential Qualities

Fundamental consciousness, as I have said, can be experienced both as emptiness and as being, or presence—a quality-rich ground. Both Buddhist and Hindu teachings describe this qualitative aspect of fundamental consciousness. Buddhism teaches that this primary dimension of ourselves has the qualities of clarity, bliss, and emptiness. Hinduism teaches that it has the attributes of truth, intelligence, and bliss (*sat-chit-ananda* in Sanskrit).

In the Realization Process, I call the qualities of fundamental consciousness awareness, emotion, and physical sensation. Although divided schematically for attunement-purposes, these qualities are a continuum. They make up the ongoing, unchanging stillness of fundamental consciousness. Specific, constantly changing awarenesses, emotions, and physical sensations pass through this unchanging quality-rich ground.

Generally, when people have not been given guidance about these qualities, they meditate in the part of themselves that is most open. People who tend to live in their emotions will usually focus in their chest when they meditate. As they continue to meditate in this way, they become increasingly emotional. People who are more mental in their stance toward life tend to meditate in their heads. They become increasingly mental as they continue their spiritual practice. This tendency to meditate in the part of your body that you most easily inhabit can intensify your imbalance and prevent you from realizing fundamental consciousness, which is a dimension of wholeness and unity. So it is very important to attune to the whole spectrum of qualities in order to realize fundamental consciousness as the basis of your whole being.

The quality of physical sensation is often the quality that is most difficult for people to access, but it is an essential aspect of our own wholeness and of our oneness with our environment. When we do not include the quality of physical sensation in our spiritual practice, we become increasingly open in the top of our body without opening the bottom of our body. This means that we feel less and less connected to the ground beneath our feet, less rooted to the earth. This upward displacement of ourselves can be very uncomfortable because we have no foundation or support for the openness in our upper body. It also cuts us off from the upward currents of energy that arise from the ground and pass through the internal space of the body. So to meditate only in our upper body not only prevents us from realizing the most subtle, unified dimension of our being, it also limits our energy dimension.

Even though we attune to each of these three essential qualities in different parts of our body, they are all everywhere in our body at once. This is easier to experience than to grasp conceptually.

EXERCISE 3 Attuning to the Qualities of Fundamental Consciousness

Sit upright on a chair or cushion, with your eyes open or closed. Feel that you are inside your whole body at once. Find the space outside your body, the space in the room. Experience that the space inside and outside your body is the same, continuous space. It pervades you. Experience that the space pervading your own body also pervades the walls of the room. Remain within your body as you experience this.

Attune to the quality of awareness around and above your head. This means becoming aware of your awareness.

Experience the quality of awareness pervading your whole body.

Experience the quality of awareness pervading your whole body and environment at the same time.

Attune to the quality of emotion in the mid-third of your body: your chest and midsection.

Experience the quality of emotion pervading your whole body.

Experience the quality of emotion pervading your whole body and environment at the same time.

Attune to the quality of physical sensation in your pelvis, legs and feet, and even below your body.

Experience the quality of physical sensation pervading your whole body.

46

Experience the quality of physical sensation pervading your whole body and environment at the same time.

Now, experience the quality of physical sensation pervading your whole body and environment, and the quality of awareness pervading your whole body and environment at the same time.

Add the quality of emotion pervading your whole body and environment. Experience all three qualities pervading your whole body and the environment at the same time. When you attune to all three qualities, they become undifferentiated from each other. It is as though they become a fourth quality that pervades everywhere. This is the qualitative feel of the presence aspect of fundamental consciousness.

Sit for a moment in this quality-rich field. Let your breath move easily through the space.

Standing and Moving as Fundamental Consciousness

Next are two of the many standing and walking exercises that we practice in the Realization Process. These exercises can help you stabilize in your realization of fundamental consciousness so that it is not a state that you go into and then lose when you move through your daily life, but is rather an ongoing way of being. Standing, walking, and moving as fundamental consciousness also help cultivate a sense of groundedness, so that you do not lose your energetic roots with the ground beneath you, and so that you can maintain the wholeness and unity of fundamental consciousness.

EXERCISE 4 Standing as Fundamental Consciousness

Stand on an even floor, preferably without wearing shoes. Experience that you are inside your feet, that you inhabit them. Let yourself experience the whole foundation that your feet provide for you, from your toes to your heels. This is not just a matter of being aware of your feet, but of actually being present within them; you *are* the internal space of your feet.

Make sure that you can continue to be in your feet as you breathe, that your inhale does not lift you up away from your feet.

Feel that there is no separation between you and the floor.

Find the centers of the bottom of your heels. Balance your awareness of these two points, finding them both at exactly the same time.

Feel that you are inside your ankles. Feel that the internal space of your ankles is continuous with the internal space of your feet.

Feel that you are inside your lower legs, knees, and thighs.

Feel that you are inside your hip sockets. Balance your awareness of the inside of your hip sockets; find them both at the same time. Feel that the hip sockets rest or settle toward the centers of the bottom of your heels. This will establish a felt connection, or subtle wiring, between the centers of your heels and your hip sockets. Feel that you are standing in your legs, rather than on them.

Feel that you are inside your whole torso: pelvis, mid-section, and chest, all the way through to the back of your torso.

Feel that you are inside your shoulders and inside your shoulder sockets. Balance your awareness of the inside of both shoulder sockets; find them both at the same time. Feel that your shoulder sockets rest on your hip sockets. This will give your shoulders and arms support.

Experience that you are inside your arms, wrists, and hands, all the way to the fingertips.

Feel that you are inside your neck, and settle into your neck. Rest in your larynx. Many people lift up, away from the ground, by pulling upward within their necks. Make sure that you are settled within your neck, so that the internal space of your neck feels related to the ground beneath you.

Feel that you are inside your head, that you inhabit your face and your whole brain.

Find the center of your head. Feel that the center of your head rests on, or settles toward, the ground.

Feel that the whole internal space of your body, including your head, is related to the ground, as if your whole body grows out of the ground.

Feel that you are inside your whole body all at once. Experience the quality of your self inside your whole body. Let yourself feel that there is no difference between your body and your self. Your self is standing there.

Now slowly lift your arms until they are straight out in front of you. Stay inside your arms and attuned to the quality of self as you move. Experience that the space within your arms is moving through the space in the room. Experience the quality of self moving through space. Lower your arms to your sides in the same way, moving through the internal space of your arms.

Bring your arms out to the side until they are perpendicular to your body. Stay inside your arms and attuned to the quality of self as you move. Bring your arms back down to your sides in the same way.

Find the space outside of your body, the space in the room. Experience that the space inside and outside your body is the same, continuous space. Feel that the space that pervades you pervades everything around you, even the walls of the room.

EXERCISE 5 Receiving the Upward Current

Find the centers of the bottom of your heels again.

Balance your awareness of these two points. Open these points to allow an upward-moving current of energy to come up from below you, into your ankles and legs. Do not draw the energy upward and do not imagine it. Open the points and allow the energy to come up by itself.

Find the inside of your hip sockets. Let the hip sockets rest toward the centers of the bottom of your heels. Receive the upward-moving energy in your hip sockets. The energy comes from below the centers of your heels.

Find the center of your head. Feel that the center of your head is settled toward the ground. Receive the upward-moving energy in the center of your head. The energy comes from below the centers of your heels and from below the center of the bottom of your torso at the same time.

Allow the upward-moving energy to continue up through the center of the crown of your head. The top of your head needs to be gently settled in order for the energy to move up through it.

The more you settle to the ground throughout your whole body, the more easily and fluidly the upward current will rise through your body.

Seeing and Hearing as Fundamental Consciousness

The way we inhabit or constrict our body determines how we see, hear, touch, smell, and taste. The body/being is a fractal pattern. A fractal is a pattern that repeats itself within a single form, on every scale within that form; for example, the shape of a tree branch mirrors the shape of the tree as a whole. The shape of an inlet along a coastland mirrors the shape of the coastline as a whole. This pattern, called self-similarity, was discovered by the mathematician Benoit Mandelbrot.[1]

In the same way, the spectrum from awareness to physical sensation that is found in the body as a whole is mirrored in each part of the body, no matter how small. Bodywork techniques such as hand or foot reflexology make use of this principle, for example, by stimulating a point in the foot that automatically stimulates a corresponding area in the rest of the body.

As I will describe more fully in the next chapter, we organize the way we live in our body in response to painful events in our childhood environment. This organization is a pattern of openness and constriction in the body that, if we do not become aware of it, becomes the shape of our being for the rest of our lives. This pattern of openness and constriction in our body as a whole is mirrored in each part of our body, no matter how small. This includes our sense organs.

So, for example, if we live mostly in the top of our body, we will look mostly out of the tops of our eyes. If we live mostly in the bottom of our bodies, we will look mostly out of the bottom of our eyes. If we live mostly in our emotions, in the middle areas of the body, we will look out of a narrow band in the middle of our eyes.

You can test this by looking at a carpet or some other fabric in the room. Paying careful attention to any changes in your body, let yourself see the texture of the carpet. You may notice that you automatically shift to the bottom of your body as you let yourself see the texture. Texture is part of our physical sensation of the world. The same shift will occur if you put your hand on a piece of fabric, and then allow yourself to feel the texture of the fabric.

When we inhabit our body as a whole, we see, hear, touch, smell, and taste with our whole body and being. This makes our experience of our environment fuller and richer. As we uncover the dimension of fundamental consciousness pervading our body and environment as a unity, our senses also become unified. We are able, for example, to see and hear at the same time. This helps produce the sense of "being in the moment" that is associated with nondual realization. We experience the present moment emerging directly out of the pervasive emptiness of fundamental consciousness as a "multimedia" experience, registering in all of our senses at once. In Buddhism, this is called direct or bare perception.

Bare perception produces a more subtle range of sensory experience. We may be able see the radiance that all forms in nature emit, or to hear that radiance as a subtle buzzing sound. We may actually see the transparency of the world pervaded by fundamental consciousness. We experience that we can see and touch, not just the surface of other people's bodies, for example, but all the way through to the being within their bodies. This is a deep, intimate experience of the world around us.

If we do not recognize, and specifically practice, this unification of the senses in fundamental consciousness, then the habitual constricted way that we use our senses will keep us in a fragmented perceptual field and prevent us from realizing the oneness of fundamental consciousness. Or we may become open in our meditation practice but we will reorganize our old pattern of perception as soon as we are engaged in our daily lives. The following is an exercise to recognize the shift that occurs in our hearing and seeing as we realize ourselves as fundamental consciousness.

EXERCISE 6 Direct Perception

Sit upright with your eyes open. Feel that you are inside your whole body at once. Find the space outside of your body, the space in the room. Now experience that the space inside and outside your body is the same, continuous space. It pervades you. Let your breath move through the space without disturbing the stillness of the space. Experience that the space that pervades your body also pervades the objects in the room and the walls of the room. Stay in your whole body as you experience this.

Experience that all of the sounds that you hear

are just occurring in the space without changing the stillness of the space. The space pervades you and the sounds.

Allow yourself to feel like the space itself is hearing the sounds. You do not have to listen in order to hear. The hearing happens by itself, without any effort on your part. Do not go out toward the sounds, but remain in your whole body as you experience this. The sounds arise directly out of the space.

Now allow everything that you see to just be in the space without changing or altering the stillness of the space. Relax your eyes and let your visual field become one with the space of fundamental consciousness.

Everything that you see, whether it is stable or moving, occurs in the space, without altering the space. The space pervades your whole body, and it pervades everything that you see.

Experience that the space itself is doing the seeing. You do not have to look in order to see. The seeing happens by itself. You are receiving the visual images, without any effort. Everything that you see arises directly out of the space.

You can practice this in front of a moving object, such as a flickering candle or steam rising from boiling water. Experience the stillness of fundamental consciousness as the visual stimulus moves through it.

Your eyes may feel unfocused as they relax. With practice, they will refocus with more clarity.

Now experience that everything you hear and everything you see occurs at the same time in the space of fundamental consciousness without disturbing it. Sit for a few minutes, letting the space do the seeing and the hearing, without any effort on your part.

The Relational Exercises

The internal space of the body has a potential that is rarely discussed in spiritual literature. It can contact and resonate with the internal space of another person's body, even across distance. As our spiritual essence, we are able to touch and be touched by another human being, all the way through the internal depth of our bodies, even without actually physically touching. The Realization Process includes exercises that two people can practice together in order to experience this potential of embodiment. When two people both attune to fundamental consciousness together, they experience that they are made of the same one consciousness, pervading them both as a unity.

The relational exercises develop the ability to relate with other people as fundamental consciousness. Since we have created most of our protective holding patterns in reaction to other people, it is important to specifically practice relating with others without losing your openness to spiritual essence. This can help you stabilize your realization, so that it is an ongoing transformation of your experience of yourself and the world.

The exercises teach how to inhabit the internal space

of your body, and the subtle core of your body, while inter-
acting with other people. The deeper the connection with
yourself, the more intimately you can connect with others
without fear of being displaced, or of losing inward attunement with yourself.

When you inhabit your body, your responses are deeper
and more fluid; for example, if you inhabit the internal space
of your chest, your emotions move more easily and deeply.
From the internal depth of yourself, you are more available
to respond to others with understanding, emotion, and
sensation. To inhabit the body means to gradually let go of
chronic rigidities. In this way, you become softer and more
open to the world around you, without losing the felt delineation between yourself and other people. The boundary
produced by inhabiting your body is distinct and permeable
at the same time.

Inhabiting your body increases the depth of your contact
with other people. If two people both inhabit their hands,
for example, and touch each other's hands, the contact of
the touch will be richer; it will extend all the way through
the internal space of each person's hand. They will feel more
than the texture of each other's skin, or the solidity of each
other's body; they will feel that they are contacting each
other's being within their hands.

As I've said, the internal space of your body is capable
of this person-to-person contact, without even requiring
actual physical contact between the two bodies; for example,
the tenderness inside your chest can feel and connect with

the tenderness inside another person's chest, from across a room. All of the qualities within your body resonate in this way with the qualities within another person's body. This resonance occurs without leaving your own body and without intruding energetically on the other person's body.

This in-depth contact can occur with anyone, even people we do not know, and people who are not attuned to the connection themselves. A woman told me recently that she was sitting on the subway and found herself connecting from the internal depth of her body to the internal depth of the people around her. She said that she was so moved by being part of this field of human love that she could barely bring herself to leave the subway at her stop. She also said that she attended a concert that same evening and noticed that she had none of the wariness that she usually felt when in a crowd.

In the following relational exercise of the Realization Process, each partner attunes to the space inside his or her own body and the body of the other person at the same time. The partners attune to the space pervading their bodies as a unity. This is not a merging with the other, not a loss of inward contact with themselves, because each person is inhabiting his or her own body.

This can help resolve some of the challenges of spiritual sensitivity. Sensitive people are often so aware of other people's mental and emotional life that they lose connection with their own inner responses and needs. They may, for example, start a relationship with someone out of an old pattern of having to take care of other people's pain, without listening to their own actual responses or level of desire for the other person. Or they may shut out a person whom they really do desire, and deprive themselves of love, so that they can maintain connection with themselves.

This relational exercise can also help partners realize their spiritual essence. Attuning to this primary essence together helps both partners deepen into the core of their being and enter into the wholeness of fundamental consciousness. In practicing these exercises, we can feel where we connect with another person and where in our bodies that connection is blocked. This can show us where the imbalances are in our own embodiment and where we are obstructing our realization of fundamental consciousness. The exercise can also help fill in the resonance between partners throughout all the qualities of their being. For example, if a couple experiences sexual and mental resonance with each other, but not emotional resonance, the exercise can help couples attune to each other emotionally.

EXERCISE 7 Couples Attunement to Fundamental Consciousness

Partners sit facing each other, upright on chairs or cushions, with eyes open. You do not have to make eye contact with each other, but keep your eyes open so that you are aware of the other person visually. Both partners follow the instructions at the same time.

Feel that you inhabit your feet. Make sure that you can stay in your feet while you breathe, that your inhale does not lift you out of your feet. Feel that you are inside your whole body at once. Find the space outside of you. Experience that the space inside and outside your body is the same, continuous space. It pervades you.

Experience that the space that pervades your body also pervades your partner. Remain in your own body as you experience this.

Let your breath pass through your own body, so that you are breathing your own location in space.

Let the space see and receive both you and your partner, just as you are in this moment. Relax your visual field so that it becomes one with fundamental consciousness.

Feel that you inhabit your brain. Find the space inside your brain and the space inside your partner's brain at the same time. This will help you feel the expanse of fundamental consciousness pervading both of you at the same time.

Attune to the quality of understanding inside your brain. Attune to your own quality of understanding and your partner's quality of understanding at the same time. This will help you feel a resonance between your own quality of understanding and your partner's quality of understanding.

Feel that you are inside your neck. Find the space

inside your neck and the space inside your partner's neck at the same time. Attune to the quality of your voice, your potential to speak, inside your neck. Attune to your own quality of voice and your partner's quality of voice at the same time.

Feel that you are inside your chest. Find the space inside your chest and the space inside your partner's chest at the same time. Attune to the quality of love inside your chest. This does not need to be a big feeling, just a little of the tenderness that you have inside your chest. Let yourself feel that you are sitting in your heart. Attune to your own quality of love and your partner's quality of love at the same time.

Feel that you are inside your midsection. Find the space inside your midsection and the space inside your partner's midsection at the same time. Attune to the quality of power, of personal strength, inside your mid-section. Attune to your own quality of power and your partner's quality of power at the same time.

Feel that you are inside your pelvis. Find the space inside your pelvis and the space inside your partner's pelvis at the same time. Attune to the quality of gender, however that feels to you, inside your pelvis. Attune to your own quality of gender and your partner's quality of gender at the same time.

Feel that you are inside your whole body at once. Attune to the quality of self inside your whole body. Attune to your own quality of self and your partner's quality of self at the same time.

Find the space outside of your body. Experience that the space inside and outside your body is the same, continuous space. It pervades you. Experience that the space that pervades you also pervades your partner. Remain in your own body as you experience this. Again, let the space see and receive you both, just as you are in this moment.

• • •

The Realization Process exercises can be combined with any other spiritual practice. Many of my students apply the exercises to martial arts or do them as a preparation for the open awareness techniques of Buddhist Vajrayana and Dzogchen meditation. If you follow a devotional path, the exercises can help you focus your mind and heart in prayer and deepen your reception of divine love.

If you do not have a meditation practice, I suggest that after each Realization Process exercise you find the subtle space of fundamental consciousness pervading you and your environment, and sit for a while as that pervasive space. As this space, you can let go of your grip on all of the content of your experience. Do not expand outward into the environment, but let yourself dissolve into the space that seems to be there already, pervading everywhere. You will not disappear because this pervasive ground is your true nature—it is who you are. Experience that the space is doing the seeing and hearing, and receiving all of your experience, just as it is in the moment.

I have taught these exercises to thousands of people, but it still amazes me to witness the transformation—as miraculous as birth—that occurs as people come home to their bodies and uncover the unified, radiant transparency pervading everywhere.

Chapter 3

Healing from
Relational Trauma

*And do not forget that the fist was also
once an open hand and fingers.*

YEHUDA AMICHAI

THE BODY IS both the arena of psychological defense
and the arena of spiritual awakening. So in the Realization
Process, we regard psychological maturity and spiritual
awakening as one and the same process. They both involve
freeing the body of the defensive holding patterns and attuning to the most subtle, primary level of being. The more
we attune to this primary level of ourselves, the easier it
becomes to recognize and release the holding patterns in our
body. As fundamental consciousness, we gradually let go of

our defensive grip on ourselves. Then we can receive the full vividness of each moment of our lives, without obstruction. We can allow the free, unguarded flow of our perceptions, cognitions, emotions, and sensations. We can experience each moment as a unified whole, inside and outside of our body at the same time.

Sometimes it is taught that spiritual awakening transcends the individual self, with its suffering and confusion. These teachings advise us to ignore the anguish of our everyday lives and to simply recognize ourselves as the vast consciousness at the foundation of our being. But no matter how clearly we may understand that our true nature is transcendent, we will not realize our true nature if we attempt to ignore our individual being. The ground of our being can only be uncovered through deep and precise contact with ourselves. The wide open space of spiritual awareness is our own mind, unbound. The wide open space of the spiritual heart is our own heart, free of constrictions.

In some contemporary spiritual teachings, the self-arising nature of fundamental consciousness is confused with the Western religious idea of grace, in which an entirely foreign but wonderful state lands on us because we have somehow pleased God. Several people have told me, sorrowfully, that they have waited and waited for this to happen, but so far have had no luck. This is not how it works. Fundamental consciousness arises when we have become open enough for it to appear. It is not something alien to us; it is our own basic nature that is revealed when our body, heart, and mind are open.

Most of the constrictions in our being are based on relational trauma. By relational trauma, I mean intolerably painful or confusing situations in our relationships with key figures in our childhood. These events can be as small as a familiar, loving face suddenly transformed by anger or tears, or as having to hold back our own tears, or voice, or vitality. If our heart hurts every time we see our mother's sad face, we may tighten our chest so that we do not feel that pain. Or if the sound of our parents arguing makes us anxious, we may tighten the anatomy involved in hearing, as well as clamping down on the anxious feeling in our stomach.

Our patterns of constriction are almost always unconscious. If they are repeated over time, they will harden in the tissues of our body and become chronic, unconscious holding patterns. These patterns become our ongoing organization of ourselves, our design of openness and defense. They become the shape of who we are, for the rest of our lives, unless we make an effort to release them. Some patterns of constriction do not become frozen in our body; they become well-traveled grooves, patterns that we go into, unconsciously, whenever present events remind us of the childhood situations that initially produced them.

There is no way that we can either limit the impact of our environment or suppress our responses to it without tightening our body. If you think of something sad and then try not to feel sad, you will find that you automatically tighten your chest. If you try not to hear the sound of a motor outside, you will automatically tighten the anatomy of your hearing.

Another way that children create their pattern of openness and defense is by mirroring their parents' pattern. This is not a conscious imitation, but rather a kind of entrainment. Living in the same energy field as our parents, we automatically resonate with the vibrational pattern of their bodies. We become open and fluid where they are open and fluid, and rigid where they are rigid.

We also form ourselves in response to contact or lack of contact with our parents. By contact, I mean the actual feeling of resonance between our own body and that of our parents. When we are children, this type of contact with our parents nurtures and matures our contact with ourselves. For example, if a mother is open in her heart but not in her pelvis, there will be a vibrational exchange between her and her child in the heart area but not in the pelvic area. The child will then grow up to be open and available in his heart, but not as open in his pelvis.

We also hold compensatory patterns in our body, such as an attitude of invulnerability or superiority. Often the compensatory pattern is layered over the pattern that expresses the trauma. A rigidly held smile, when released, may reveal a chronic expression of sorrow and loss. A posture of expansion or inflation may mask a deflated posture of humiliation. The compensatory patterns may also become rigid, unconscious shapes within our body, or they may be more fluid: patterns that we unconsciously move into when we are threatened in similar ways to the threats in our childhood.

The constrictions that become frozen in the body contain within them the memory, age, and emotions of the traumatic situations. I worked with a woman who had organized herself to withstand a severely neglectful childhood environment by constricting her solar plexus, chest, and head. As she began to recognize and release these constrictions from her body, she remembered the actual feel of herself as a young child, the emotional coldness and sense of deadness that seemed to permeate the house, the weight of her mother's depression as she lay on her bed upstairs, the threat of her father's drunken state as he secluded himself in the kitchen. She felt the mental disorientation, longing, desolation, and anxiety that she had suppressed as a child. These feelings would have been intolerable for her as a child; they might even have overwhelmed her sanity. Now, as an adult, she was able both to observe and to feel them at the same time. She could allow these feelings to register in her adult consciousness without overwhelming her, and then discharge them from her body.

Since we tend to revisit the same protective patterns during similar relational traumas, most of our holding patterns contain layers of different memories, emotions, and ages; for example, a chronic pattern of constriction in one's neck in response to being fed against one's will may also be evoked by smothering affection from a parent. Both of these relational memories may emerge in the process of recognizing and releasing this pattern from the body.

Even if these primal traumas and holding patterns are now rigid, static areas of the body, they also contain the specific pathways of the movement into the constriction. As we will see, this becomes important in the process of releasing them.

Our static defensive patterns fragment our experience of ourselves and our environment. According to neuroscientists such as Joseph LeDoux, traumas cause a split between the cognitive and affective functions of the brain, specifically between the amygdala/hippocampus loop that mediates emotion and the ventromedial prefrontal cortex that regulates and makes sense of emotional experience.[1]

Psychologists, such as Elizabeth Howell in her book *The Dissociative Mind,* describe the effects of relational trauma as the splitting of one part of the personality from other parts, and as a kind of overall numbing of oneself, a sense of being not quite real.[2] They say that the inability to accept or to fully encompass a traumatic experience produces dissociative patterns that obstruct our subjective sense of wholeness.

When we include the body in our understanding of trauma, we see that the subjective sense of wholeness is not solely a mental phenomenon. It is based on actual contact with the whole internal space of one's body. Our psychological holding patterns constrict or fragment our ability to inhabit our body, so that we cannot experience ourselves as a whole. This is what produces the sense of numbness, or being not quite present or real.

We compensate for this lack of experience with abstract ideas about ourselves. This is often called "living in one's head." Usually, the constrictions in the body also keep us from inhabiting our whole head or our whole brain. We do not live in our head, but we do live in our ideas. We go about life *thinking* about ourselves rather than *experiencing* ourselves. We may think: I am a teacher, or I am a generous person, or I am an unworthy person. These ideas shift according to our circumstances, especially in relation to the way we think that other people are responding to us. So we may think "I am an intelligent, superior person" in one circumstance, and "I am an idiot" in another circumstance. Or we define ourselves by our preferences, or our culture, or our profession.

As we are able to inhabit the body, our abstract sense of self is replaced with an actual experience of ourselves, with an experience of the essential qualities of our being. We can say that this is a qualitative sense of self, rather than a narrative sense of self. The qualities of our being—the actual feel of our intelligence, love, power, and gender— are always there within the body. When we experience these qualities, we feel real.

How Many Selves?

The concept of multiple selves has recently become popular in the field of psychology. Howell, for example, writes that we normally fragment ourselves into various relatively fixed ways of behaving in response to different situations.[3] We may be humble and shy in relation to authority figures, but bossy and demanding in our intimate relationships. These various "self states," as Howell refers to them, make up our constructed personality.

If these aspects of our personality are rigidly cut off from each other, then psychologists say that we have a dissociative disorder. Having an overall sense of our personality and being able to switch fluidly from one self state to another is considered the normal condition of the human psyche. In other words, the direction of psychological health is toward harmony among our variety of self states, and away from rigid fragmentation.

However, inhabiting the body enables us to view our behavior from a unified perspective. We will still respond and behave differently with different people, or in different situations, but these passing variations will not affect the underlying steadiness of our unified, authentic sense of self. In other words, we will always know ourselves as a whole, even when we are expressing just a small fraction of our personality. I believe that the direction of psychological health goes even further than harmony between self states; it goes toward an embodied, unified, qualitative contact with ourselves.

Trauma and the Realization Process

All of the Realization Process exercises cultivate the ability to inhabit one's body as a whole. This heals the split between our cognitive abilities and our emotional experience. We can then more easily make sense of our early traumas, as well as any painful events in our current lives. We can also observe, experience, express, and act in the world as our whole self at once.

Inhabiting the body develops a sense of self-possession, and a sense of there being someone "at home." It may initially feel challenging to be present in one's body, especially if we attempted to be invisible as children in order to avoid a parents' anger or abuse. But when we are able to live within our body, we experience it as much safer than not being there. Inhabiting the body produces an internal sense of volume, of taking up space. This provides some weight or substance to the sense of self that is empowering, even in difficult situations with other people. The internal sense of volume also acts as a kind of buffer against abrasive stimuli. People report that they feel less like life is impinging directly on them. They feel less "thin-skinned," less susceptible to the force of environmental stimuli.

In this way, the experience of inner volume, and of having internal space in which to live, creates a felt delineation between I and not-I. This delineation is based on the natural internal coherence that occurs as we realize fundamental consciousness pervading our whole body. It is not something that we have to guard or reinforce. When we experience life from within the body rather than from its surface, we find that we can relax our protective vigilance to the world around us.

As I explained in the last chapter, the Realization Process exercise of attuning to fundamental consciousness (exercise 1, page 34) also attunes to the essential qualities within the body. This exercise is particularly helpful for people who hold negative ideas about themselves based on traumatic childhood wounding, or based on recent attacks such as rape. People who were sexually abused as children, for example, often have a sense of shame about these assaults, even though they were the victims. Some people who were abused as children have described themselves to me as "garbage" or "damaged goods." To experience the actual qualities of one's own aliveness can help people relinquish these negative beliefs. To experience that there is love within one's chest, even when we are alone, makes it difficult for us to continue to feel hatred for ourselves. To feel the actual quality of one's intelligence makes it difficult for us to continue to think of ourselves as stupid, or to feel overwhelmed by the minds of other people. To experience the quality of power in one's body goes a long way toward healing the feelings of shame and vulnerability that we may harbor from having been overpowered in our childhood. One survivor of childhood sexual abuse told me, after some practice of inhabiting her body, that she felt "sweet" inside. This sense of innate sweetness helped her develop a belief in her own value and to finally break her pattern of attraction to abusive partners. It also helped her to have compassion for herself and to see her self-destructive behaviors as the result of the damage that was done to her.

The exercise of the core breath (exercise 2, page 41) can also help increase our sense of safety. From the core of the body, we experience our environment from a deeper perspective. Many people who were traumatized as children, and who have fairly severe dissociation as adults, have a diffuse energetic quality. Their energy seems to leak out and dissolve in the space around them. They seem too loose, as if the center of their being has given way, or as if they have abandoned themselves and tried to disappear into the atmosphere. This vanishing act is one of the main defenses that children automatically employ when being attacked physically and/or sexually. If repeated over time, this defensive pattern becomes a way of being. As we will see in later chapters of this book, if a child is particularly sensitive or open, they may react in this way to their childhood environment even if they are not severely abused.

The core breath exercise can help us feel gathered and secure within the innermost core of our being, so that we feel present all the way through our body. The subtle core of the body is our entranceway into the oneness of fundamental consciousness, but it is also the deepest contact that we can have with our individual self. By living within the subtle core of the body, we can experience intimate connection with other people without feeling overpowered or annihilated by them.

Pattern Recognition and Release Exercises

The Realization Process also works directly with the holding patterns in the body, to both recognize and release them. Through the interface of our mind, energy system, and connective tissue, we can bind any aspect of our being, such as our perception, emotional responses, or capacity for understanding. These holding patterns may reside deeply within the body and be invisible to an observer and cut off from our own consciousness. They can only be uncovered through sensitive attunement to the internal space of the body.

Even the most rigidly held of these patterns are frozen moments of movement; they contain the repetitive movement into the pattern before it became hardened into a static shape, as well as the reverse pathway into release. Also, all of these patterns will move a little, they will intensify, as we talk about the events that first produced them. A carefully attentive listener can observe this "dance of veils" as someone talks to them about their childhood. These movements may be quite subtle and occur within the internal space of the body while not actually moving the surface of the body. There may be a slight pulling inward of the chest that is barely visible, but which limits emotional responsiveness. There may be a slight pulling inward of one side of a person's head that was the person's reaction to verbal or physical assault. Therapists trained in the Realization Process are attuned to the space that pervades both their own body and the client's body, so that holding patterns and subtle movements within the body can be observed.

One of the ways in which the Realization Process helps to release holding patterns is by finding the pattern from the subtle core of the body. We find the center of our head (the center of the internal space of the head, between the ears), and from the center of the head, we find the area of tension within the body. Finding the holding pattern from the center of the head helps to penetrate into the subtle depth of the tension. Then, holding our focus within the tension, we breathe within the center of our head. As we do this, there will usually be a spontaneous movement within the tension, either toward an intensification of the holding pattern, or toward release. We are not making a volitional movement into the constriction, but rather we are focusing within the constriction and allowing it to move by itself.

When the pattern moves toward intensification, it is often possible to recognize what the holding pattern is expressing or reacting to, along with the memory of the event (or events) that produced the holding pattern, the emotional charge contained within the pattern, and even the quality of the age (or ages) that we were when we moved into that pattern. We may even find the fragment of childhood mentality that is aligned with the movement.

When the pattern has moved as far as possible into the constriction, it will move spontaneously toward release. With practice, the defensive movement becomes increasingly fluid and increasingly conscious, until it gradually releases completely. This is a very subtle process. It is not a volitional movement or defensive gesture. Rather, it is an inward observation of this fragment of ourselves—of our body, heart, and mind—as it follows its actual pathway into constriction and release.

It is important that we inhabit the internal space of the body that has been freed by the letting go of the holding pattern, that we claim this new internal territory. In this way, the exercise of inhabiting the body can help maintain the release of the pattern.

Another Realization Process exercise, explained more fully in chapter 7, can help us recognize how we have constricted ourselves in relation to the important people in our childhood. In this practice, we imagine a parent, for example, in the space in front of us. Then we feel that we inhabit our whole body, and that the space that pervades our body also pervades this image. We bring our attention to the space pervading our parent's head and notice any changes that occur within our own body as we do this. Then we bring our attention to the space pervading our parent's neck, chest, midsection, and pelvis, each time feeling any shifts that occur within our own body. This exercise can reveal how we have protected ourselves from our parents, and also how we have mirrored them. It can also help us feel the deep bonds of love between ourselves and our parents.

This exercise provides an effective basis for understanding our early relationships, and even for finding compassion for ourselves and our parents. I worked with a woman whose father had never expressed love for her. She was both bitterly angry at him and critical of herself, feeling that she must be in some way flawed and unlovable. But when she attuned to the space pervading the image of her father's chest, she could feel how constricted he was, and she could even feel the wounded child that he had been. Then she knew that he had done the best that he could in loving her, and that there was not anything wrong with her. She was able to forgive both him and herself for the limitations in that relationship, and to feel love for him without needing him to be different than he was.

Complete freedom from these trauma-based constrictions in the body is an ideal, but we do not have to be completely free to be able to inhabit the internal space of our body. As the major holding patterns in our body release, we are able to make inward contact with ourselves. Long before we have released all of our holding patterns, if we ever do, we become open enough throughout our body to uncover our basic identity: subtle, fundamental consciousness, pervading inside and outside of ourselves as a whole. As this basic transparency, it becomes increasingly easy to recognize and release the holding patterns from our body, which in turn allows us to become even more open throughout our body. So even after we have stabilized in our realization of inner and outer unity, we can continue to open to the vast spaciousness of fundamental consciousness.

EXERCISE 8 Releasing Binding from the Subtle Core of the Body

Find a place in your body where you feel there is an area of tension.

Find the center of your head.

From the center of your head, bring your focus deep within the tension in your body.

Keeping your focus there, breathe normally through your nose. Let yourself be open to any feelings, thoughts, memories, or images that may occur as you do this.

Attune to the emotional tone of the tension. See if you can feel which emotion (if any) is held within the tension. How old do you feel as you experience this emotional tone? If you are remembering yourself at some time in your past, what is happening around you in this memory?

You can also attune to the tension in such a way that you experience a spontaneous movement toward the constricted position. In other words, you are experiencing exactly how you moved in order to close this part of your body. This is not a volitional movement, but an observation of a spontaneous movement within your body.

As you do this, you may also be able to feel what the movement is expressing, or what you are holding back or protecting yourself against. Then let go and allow the constriction to release. Repeat this movement into the constriction and release several times. The release will happen little by little. With repeated practice, the movement into the constriction will become both more fluid and more conscious. Eventually, it will let go completely.

PART TWO

Spiritual
Sensitivity

Chapter 4

Thin Skin: The Challenge of Becoming Resilient

MOST PEOPLE DO not come to their first session with me bearing gifts, but Eva did. She thrust her hand through the door before she entered, so that I saw the gift before I met her. It was a bouquet of spiky yellow straw flowers, wrapped in white tissue paper. Eva arrived a moment later—a tall, angular woman with coal-black hair and alert but guarded blue eyes. When she handed me the bouquet, one of the flower heads broke off and hung crookedly from its stalk, and Eva glanced at me apprehensively.

I set the flowers carefully on a side table and invited her to sit on the couch facing my chair. Her wariness seemed to abate a little as she sat and focused squarely on my face for a long moment. She did not seem to be observing me so much as listening for something, as if she might receive word from the silence of my good and bad qualities. When she finally spoke, I was surprised at the timid politeness of her voice. "Do you mind very much if I sit over there?" she asked, motioning to another chair. When she had moved, and I had turned my chair to face her, she explained apologetically, "I just can't look at that painting right now." The print on the wall behind my chair was a brightly colored abstract with a lot of movement in it.

Now Eva closed her eyes and sat for a long time without moving. She seemed to be focusing on her breath, or even willing herself to breathe. I waited for some sign that she was ready to begin, until finally I became concerned that we would pass the whole hour in this way. "Eva," I said softly, "what would you like from the session?"

She opened her eyes slowly and met my gaze, still breathing in the same studied rhythm. For a moment, I was allowed a clear view through the blue shimmer of her eyes. Then abruptly I was shut out; her eyes transformed to flat disks. Now I saw that the surface of her whole body seemed taut, as if she wore a thin coat of varnish, brittle and opaque.

"I've seen so many therapists," she said, pronouncing the name of my profession with distaste. "I know all about my critical father and my needy mother. It doesn't help, hasn't helped me at all. I still feel overwhelmed. I still can't walk down the street and feel like a normal person, can't read a newspaper headline without, you know." Her eyes brimmed suddenly with tears, at some painful memory. "I can't stand the noise of the cars outside my house, or the buzz of my computer, or the high-pitched sound of the heating system in my room when I'm trying to concentrate." Her words stopped abruptly, as if she had no hope that I would understand them. She gazed out the window across the room and seemed to drift into the street, leaving her rigid, vacant form folded protectively on the chair. I had the sense that she was soothing herself among the trees outside.

As if reading my mind, she said, "I only feel real when I'm in nature. It's like I can hear the trees speaking . . . I don't mean with words." Eva stopped and listened keenly to the silence for my reaction. "You will probably think I'm crazy, but I don't think that I am. I can feel the life inside the trees; it's like a voice. I guess it's the only voice that seems gentle enough." With that, she managed to tighten her varnish-like surface, becoming as still and remote as a statue, consigning me to the coarse, unnatural world of human beings.

We sat for a while in the silence. I relaxed the bit of anxiety that had been building in my chest, and I felt Eva relax at the same time. I suddenly became aware of the whirring of the white noise machine outside my office door, and I went to turn it off. When I returned to my chair, Eva had also returned her presence to the room.

"What I want from the session is to be able to live in the world as myself," she said.

Sensory Sensitivity

Spiritually sensitive people have often lived, since earliest childhood, with a particularly subtle attunement to the world around them. Sensory stimuli, such as colors or sounds or smells, impact them with unusual intensity.

Although this sensitivity is a source of enjoyment, it may also cause extreme discomfort. Sensitive people often have low tolerance for abrasive stimuli. They feel that life impinges directly on them, that they cannot establish any distance, or any barrier, between themselves and their environment. They often describe themselves as somehow "flimsier" than other people. They feel that they do not have enough substance of their own to hold up against the abrasive forces around them. They can feel displaced by a loud sound or a vivid color, or by the presence of another person. The sounds of a city street, the inflections of other people's voices, even the supposed white noise of the various motors from their household appliances may disrupt their ability to sense their own internal life, their own thoughts and feelings.

People with exceptional sensory sensitivity often become agitated in stimulating environments that can be easily tolerated by other people. A party or an exciting movie, for example, can rattle them for days afterward. They may also notice small nuances in the facial expressions or vocal tones of other people. "Just to hear someone say hello," a friend once told me, "is like a symphony played by a full orchestra." In this way, sensitivity can produce an effect similar to trauma, by overwhelming the nervous system.

Many sensitive people live in a chronic state of overstimulation. This means that they almost never quite relax. They are always, to some extent, "on edge."

In order to avoid feeling annihilated by another person, they may avoid forming close relationships. Or they may connect with other people by sacrificing inward attunement to their own emotions, thoughts, desires, and needs. Their relationships are often fraught with conflict between their need for intimacy and their need to know and express themselves.

But sensitivity, the capacity to see deeply into other people and things, and to be deeply touched and moved by them, is synonymous with the capacity for contact and intimacy. This can be a frustrating dilemma for sensitive people. The more capable they are of contact with the world around them, the less tolerance they may have for the stimulation of that contact.

It may also be challenging to be in relationship with extremely sensitive people. They may seem unresponsive to affection, for example, when they are actually protecting themselves against overstimulation. They may need to be approached more slowly and carefully than other people, especially when initiating sexual intimacy with them. Recently, a woman complained to me that her husband just reaches out and touches her breast when he wants to be intimate. Her husband was bewildered by this complaint, saying that most women like to have their breasts touched. But he learned that she was capable of feeling intense pleasure at his touch when he began by touching her more lightly and gently.

The Research

Psychologist Elaine Aron, in her research on highly sensitive people, found that 15 to 20 percent of the population she interviewed described themselves as extremely sensitive. Aron writes that sensitivity is the ability to notice more than other people do, and to reflect on the information more deeply.[1]

With the exception of Aron, much of the current literature on sensitivity discusses sensitivity as a problem, as a disorder of the nervous system. A popular line of research about sensitivity highlighted in Carol Kranowitz's book *The Out-of-Sync Child*, is based on the work of Dr. A. Jean Ayres. It describes some of the difficulties faced by sensitive people as "sensory processing disorder" or "sensory integration disorder."[2] While many sensitive people suffer from some of the same results of overstimulation mentioned by sensory processing therapists (such as being easily distracted or disoriented, and disliking loud sounds or "itchy" clothing fabric), the sensitivity that I am describing is not in itself a disorder. It is a gift, a marker of spiritual potential. Unlike the array of symptoms mentioned in the sensory processing literature, the people who have this gift are usually well-coordinated and high functioning.

Traditional psychologists sometimes interpret extreme sensitivity, and the resulting tendency toward isolation and tenuous connection with one's own internal life, as an indication of early and/or severe psychological wounding. For the most part, however, these sensitive individuals do not suffer the symptoms associated with severe psychological disturbance; for example, they are often particularly capable of empathy and of unselfish concern for other people, and of understanding and tolerating contradictions in other people's behavior. They often express deep, authentic emotion, and the ability for complex, abstract thought.

Reading Nature's Fine Print

I have found that in addition to the ability to notice more in their environment, sensitive people sometimes have access to a subtle range of perception that also does not rely on the actual acuity of the senses, such as "20/20 vision." The senses become increasingly refined and "transpersonal" with spiritual maturity; for example, the revered Indian sage Ramakrishna had such a refined sense of touch that he cried out when he saw a cow being whipped, because he could actually feel (not just imagine) the animal's pain.

People with heightened sensitivity may detect a subtle range of sensory phenomena that can be described as "vibratory." They may see light or color emanating from people, animals, and plants, or hear the subtle buzz of energy fields in the air surrounding them. Some can put their hands on a tree or plant and feel the life force moving within it, or even sense this movement without physical touch. Or they can discern physical pain, tensions, or specific emotions within another person's body. They may sense the vibrations of people's emotions and intentions even when these are at odds with their facial expressions or vocal tones. Some possess extrasensory perception (ESP), the ability to transmit and receive information in ways that seem entirely independent of the conventional use of the senses. I worked with a body therapist who was able to hear the words of my thoughts and repeat them to me verbatim. This rich and sometimes contradictory sensory and emotional world can be overwhelming and confusing, especially for a child. It may also alienate the child from family members and peers who find the child's perceptions strange or even threatening.

Also in this subtle range of perception are inner visions, usually seen in one's forehead or in the space just in front of one's forehead. These may be geometric shapes such as concentric circles or triangles, or faces or figures, or they can be images of future events or information about other people. Unlike hallucinations, these sensory experiences are not the product of the imagination and they do not represent or express the traumas of the seer's childhood. Sensitive people see, hear, and sense stimuli that are actually present as subtle aspects of nature.

Some sensitive people find their subtle sensory experiences to be alarming and disorienting, especially if they emerge suddenly. I worked with a woman who began to see light in the air. For many months, until she became used to her new degree of sensitivity, she found this light so distracting that she would try to bat it away with her hands.

Becoming More Sensitive

Although sensitivity may cause discomfort, it is an entranceway into life's spiritual dimension. Sensitive people sometimes try to make themselves more solid or dense, or to shut themselves off from the onslaught of stimuli in their daily lives. However, the cure for this discomfort is actually to become more sensitive and open. As you continue to develop your sensitivity, your consciousness can become so refined that it is finally the luminous transparency of fundamental consciousness, pervading the material world. When this happens, stimuli can move through this dimension of consciousness without disturbing it. As fundamental consciousness, you remain steady and open while the movement of life flows through you. This means that you can continue to become even more subtly attuned to life without being overwhelmed by the world around you.

Attunement to fundamental consciousness also helps you tolerate stimuli in your environment because it requires you to inhabit your body. When you live within your body, you have a felt sense of internal depth and wholeness. You can also feel the qualities of your being, such as your love, understanding, and power. This is an experience of actually existing, and of possessing yourself from the inside. This internal depth, wholeness, and quality of being cannot be broken. Stimuli move through it without altering it.

As your senses become refined—as you reach the subtle range of your senses—they also become unified. The vibrational nature of reality that is revealed with your subtle senses is seen/heard/touched/smelled/tasted all at once. Finally, as you realize yourself as fundamental consciousness, you have a single, direct experience of each moment. All sensory stimuli seem to emerge directly out of the pervasive empty spaciousness of your consciousness, without any effort on your part. This produces the feeling of immediacy or "nowness" that is associated with spiritual experience.

Beginning the Work

In my second meeting with Eva, I began to teach her the first exercise of the Realization Process, attuning directly to fundamental consciousness by inhabiting the internal space of the body. As I explained in chapter 1, to inhabit your body is different than becoming aware of your body. It means that you actually live within your body; you feel that you *are* the internal space of yourself.

Most people live on the surface of themselves or even outside of their body. They experience their environment from this external perspective. This is particularly true of very sensitive people who have held a lifelong hypervigilant stance toward their environment. Their alertness to visual and audible stimuli unbalances their focus toward the external world. If their childhood environment was at all threatening or unpredictable, this pattern will be augmented by fear. They will not feel safe to focus inwardly; they may be afraid that something terrible will happen if they relax their vigilance toward the atmosphere around them.

However, when we live on the protective surface of ourselves, the world seems to impinge directly on us. Paradoxically, when we dissolve that rigid boundary and live within the internal space of our body, life can impact us even more deeply, without displacing or annihilating us.

As explained in chapter 2, the attunement to fundamental consciousness begins with a breathing exercise that can help you contact yourself inwardly. This is done by inhaling through your nose and bringing your inhale breath straight back through the internal space of your head. The exhale is simply a release.

This breath has two purposes: The first is learning to direct the breath inward. Directing the breath straight back through your head cultivates the ability to penetrate inward, to burrow through what may be the unknown inner depths of your body. This is a preparation for being able to contact and inhabit the inner depths of your body.

The second purpose of this breathing exercise is to refine the breath. When you live within your body, your breath becomes more subtle. It does not just engage your physical respiratory system; it reaches everywhere in your body at once. This breathing exercise provides the very beginning of that refinement.

After I had instructed Eva in this inward breath, I continued with the exercise. I said, "Feel that you are inside the internal space of your feet, that you inhabit your feet."

I looked down at Eva's long, narrow feet perched rigidly on the floor.

"Let your feet soften," I suggested, "so that you can sink deeply inside of them. Especially soften the area of your feet right in front of your ankles, and relax your toes."

The instruction to inhabit one's body is a strange one for many people, and some interpret it as asking them to visualize themselves inside their feet. "Am I sitting or lying down inside my feet?" they ask, reasonably. But Eva seemed to understand what I was after, for her feet did soften, and I saw the whole internal space of her feet become alive with her presence.

"Now attune to the quality of your self, inside your feet."

This instruction is also unusual, of course, and people sometimes stop the exercise right here and want me explain what I mean. Attuning to the quality of self within the body is a very direct means of entering into the most subtle dimension of yourself. As I've mentioned, it is experienced as a particular, specific quality within your whole body that feels like the quality of "self." In other words, it feels like what we have always known, in the background of all our experience, as our self. Even though we recognize it as the quality of our own self, it is the same quality in everyone. By attuning to the quality of self even in one part of our body, such as the feet, we begin to awaken to the whole internal depth of ourselves as a unity. So this quality of self is an entranceway into the wholeness of our essential being.

Eva easily attuned to the quality of self in her feet. Although we have no words to describe such a qualitative shift, it is a change that can be experienced in yourself and that can also be seen by a sensitive observer.

"Now feel that you are inside your ankles and lower legs," I continued.

But Eva was not ready to move from the internal space of her feet. A look of amazement had come over her face, and she held up a hand to stop my instructions, as if any verbal communication might break the spell. We sat for a long time while Eva became acquainted with the internal space of her feet. Finally she opened her eyes and said to me softly, but with some authority, "That's enough for today."

The experience of inhabiting her body, and the exhilarating sensation of her own existence, was so intense for Eva that she could only approach it gradually. Each session she was able to go a little further with the exercise, inhabiting more of her body. I remember the expression of solemn concentration on her face as she entered into each new part of herself, breathing carefully as if she were savoring a delicate elixir.

It took six sessions for Eva to be able to inhabit all of the parts of her body. After inhabiting each part of the body separately, the exercise goes on to inhabiting the whole internal space of the body at once. For people who have always lived, as most people have, on the surface of themselves, it is a relief to find that they have this internal chamber in which to reside. Instead of knowing yourself just as the thin, vulnerable interface with a rough and sometimes threatening world, you have the capacity to know yourself all the way through the internal substance of yourself.

Here and There: The Same Space

As Eva inhabited her whole body for the first time, her face became transfixed with almost excruciating pleasure. Having become familiar by now with her pace, I waited several minutes before going on with the exercise, watching her slowly acclimate herself to the intensity of this new experience. When I asked her to attune to the quality of self in her whole body, she tensed for a moment.

"Will I disappear?" she whispered to me. "No," I assured her, "you will be even more present than before." As Eva attuned to the quality of self, she seemed to glow from within. The sharp angles of her body now seemed rounded and soft. It looked like an inward ripening, as if something that had been dormant and hard had now become soft and vital.

"That's right," she said, "I'm really here. This is me."

"Keeping your eyes closed," I continued, "find the space outside of your body, the space in the room." Eva's powerful radar swept through the room.

"Now feel that the space inside and outside your body is the same, continuous space. It pervades you. You are still in your body, but you are permeable, transparent. The space inside and outside of your body is the same, continuous space."

For many people, this instruction is not necessary. Just by inhabiting the whole internal space of the body, the sense of boundary between internal and external experience dissolves. To inhabit our body as a whole spontaneously uncovers the very subtle, unified, fundamental consciousness that pervades our body and our surroundings at the same time. In practical terms, this means that we can experience internal cohesion and deep internal contact with ourselves at the same time as we experience connection to the world around us. As fundamental consciousness, our attention to inner and outer experience is completely balanced.

As Eva attuned to the space pervading her body and environment at the same time, she became even more radiant and transparent, as if she were made of a fine light. She also seemed to become calmer, settling more deeply within her body.

"Eva," I went on with the exercise, "slowly open your eyes. We have a few more steps to do with the eyes open."

After several moments, Eva's eyelids began to flicker, and very slowly, she opened her eyes. When she saw me sitting in front of her, however, she shut them again.

"That's okay," I said, getting up and moving across the room. "I'll stand over here, out of your eye range, so that you can look straight in front of you." That was easier said than done, as Eva's "eye range," when she opened her eyes again, seemed to encompass the whole room. I finally flattened myself against the furthest wall, and she focused on my empty chair in front of her.

"Now with your eyes open," I continued, "experience that you are inside your whole body at once."

I knew that this would be extremely challenging for someone as sensitive to her surroundings as Eva. "Try to maintain internal contact with yourself," I said, "as you experience the room around you. Even though the world appears, you still have your own temple to sit in."

The idea of her own temple seemed to make sense to her. She settled within herself and became somehow rounder and fuller.

"Now find the space outside your body, the space in the room. Feel that the space inside and outside your body is the same, continuous space."

Like many people, Eva could feel the space pervading her surroundings and all of her body, except for her head. It was as if she was keeping her head removed so that she could observe the attunement. "Let the space pervade you completely," I said, "even your head, so that you are completely immersed in this pervasive space."

Finally she surrendered her head to the transparency and openness of fundamental consciousness. As fundamental consciousness, we do not need to separate ourselves from our experience in order to observe it. Our observing capacity and experiencing capacity become unified.

Then I went on. "Eva, I'm going to stay here, against the wall. Without looking at me, see if you can feel that the space that pervades you also pervades me."

In a flash, I felt Eva's attention leave her body and enter mine. "Stay in your body," I cautioned. "You do not have to move at all from inside your own body to feel that the space pervades us both. It's just a settling into the space that seems to already be there, pervading everything."

Although these instructions may seem strange, I have found that almost everyone I teach has been able to follow them. The pervasive space of fundamental consciousness seems to already be there. We do not create it or imagine it. After a while, we do not even have to attune to it. Although these exercises are volitional acts of attunement, eventually we can simply let go into this subtle dimension. It occurs spontaneously: a transparency of our own being and everything around us. Fundamental consciousness is our most relaxed state, because it is the part of ourselves that is beyond any contrivance or imagination. It is who we really are. But as I have said, if we just let go into this space without inhabiting our body, we will probably just let go from the surface of ourselves. In order to let go into our most subtle spiritual essence, we need to experience it pervading our body and environment at the same time.

Eva looked surprised for a moment, but she was able to settle into the space-like consciousness that pervaded my body without leaving her own. She suddenly looked over and smiled at me warmly. It was her first acknowledgement of the bond that had been growing between us in the past weeks. Feeling connected with herself and with me at the same time gave her the sense of safety she needed to express her warm feelings for me. I smiled, too.

"Now one more step," I said. "Feel that the space that pervades your body also pervades the walls of the room. That's how subtle it is; it even pervades the walls, the floor, the ceiling. Again, you do not need to move at all from within your body in order to experience this."

When she had sat for a few minutes in this pervasive space, I asked, "How does that feel?"

Eva was silent for a long moment. Then she said, "It feels very tender, as if I have just been born." Then, suddenly, she became brittle and opaque again. "But how do I keep this tender feeling out in the street," she asked, "or when I'm with other people?"

Transparency In Action

Although this deep essence of ourselves does feel tender and soft, it also feels substantial, like existence itself. In Buddhism, it is described as diamond-hard and indestructible. In fact, this very subtle dimension cannot be damaged in any way. In Zen Buddhism, this space is described as "I have never moved from the beginning." It has always been there, at the core of our being, even before we realized it. Also, attunement to this openness is based on deep internal contact with our own being. So this tenderness is receptive and responsive, but it is also strong and secure.

I suggested to Eva that she practice inhabiting her body whenever she was in a public place, like a restaurant or movie theater, or at work. I wanted her to feel secure within her own body before she practiced attuning to space pervading herself and her environment, out in the world.

Eva was a graphic designer at an advertising agency. She had mentioned to me that she was thinking of quitting her job, because she felt that her coworkers disapproved of her. She often had the sense that they were speaking about her behind her back. But she also acknowledged that she had often felt this way in other work environments, and that she tended to not to stay very long at any one job for that reason. It is common for sensitive people to feel extremely self-conscious about their differences from other people, and even to misread people's facial expressions as disapproval or ridicule.

After practicing for several weeks, she reported to me that she had experienced a breakthrough. She had attended a staff meeting, a monthly event that had always been "unbearable" for her. She described how she usually felt either invisible or too conspicuous among the other staff members.

"But this week, I felt something I've never felt before in my life," she said. "I felt that I took up space." Excitement moved through her body as she spoke, and she put her hands on her chest as if to contain it. "At the meeting, I realized that there was a place for me to be. I was here in my body, and everyone else was outside of my body. Does this make sense? Ha! I exist because I take up space, I can feel myself taking up space.

"And I kept attuning to the feeling of love inside my chest," she continued. "I said to myself, 'I'm a good person, I have this love inside my chest. It doesn't matter what they think of me.' And then I actually started to notice more who they are, rather than who they think I am."

After several months, I noticed a change in Eva. Her body had softened even more, and the sharp angles of her long limbs seemed more harmonious. Her eyes had lost some of their opacity. She seemed to settle within herself instead of drifting out of her body, but there was still something insular and protective about the way she held herself.

I asked her how it was going at work. "Oh, much better," she said. "I'm really holding my own there, now. I'm setting boundaries, closing the door to my office whenever it gets too noisy in the hallway. Before I was always afraid they would think I was weird if I did that."

"That's great, Eva. But do you still feel a little isolated there?"

Eva was silent for a long time. As in our first session, she seemed to be testing the atmosphere in the room for its trustworthiness. Finally, she said, "They all seem to know how to talk to each other, they all listen to the same music, and go to the same movies. I just feel different."

Eva's voice carried more emotion than usual as she said this. Instead of her usual soft, thoughtful tone, she sounded angry, defiant, and sad. She looked suddenly like a young child, around eight or nine, confused and terribly lonely.

For the first time since we had begun working together, we spent the session talking about her childhood. She was the oldest child, but her two siblings were born when she was still quite young. She remembered them crying all the time, and then as they got older, their boisterous play in the house. She had always felt bothered by the sounds of the family in their small apartment and stayed alone in her room with the door closed as much as she could. Even in her room, she remembers feeling bombarded by the sounds and smells of the city that came in through her window. When she went to school, she also felt like an outsider. The other children seemed "too big, too loud"; even the way they moved and shoved each other and ran around during recess alarmed her.

Eva was able to feel how she had "hardened her skin" to separate herself from them. She had also discovered that if she held herself very still, the sounds and movement around her could not "get inside" her. Now she could feel how this rigid stillness also kept her from experiencing herself.

I suggested that she was ready to practice feeling space pervade her and the other people at work. She would still be in her body, but she would not be cut off from contact with the people around her. I reminded her that she was able to experience that with me quite well.

"But it's very different here with you," she protested. "It's quiet here; you're quiet. And you're careful with me. These other people aren't careful. I don't want to be in the same space with them." She seemed astounded by her own outburst, which had built to a furious pitch as she spoke. "Wow," she said. "I'm really angry at them, and I don't even really know them. It's like I'm angry at the world." She looked over at me warily and I nodded. We both knew that she had recognized something important about herself.

Before she could live in the openness of pervasive consciousness, she would have to come to terms with her anger toward the abrasive world. For Eva, it was a process of forgiveness. In the next few weeks, she struggled to forgive her brothers for being so loud when they were children, and her coworkers for living in a sensory realm that was different from her own. She spoke about forgiving the media, and even the artists and musicians for their garish designs and their loud, monotonous music. She finally confronted her anger toward her parents for never understanding her sensitivity.

I listened as she thrashed through her painful feelings of anger and shame, and as she began to find a sense of compassion for herself and for the world around her. There was no way to separate the psychological from the spiritual in this deep healing of herself. She had to retrace the lines of her personal history to her earliest memories of recoiling from the abrasive environment in order to understand and cease her automatic recoil from life today. She had to become aware of the very unpleasant sensations that she had held in her body since childhood, such as disgust and helpless overwhelm, so that they no longer motivated her responses to the world.

It slowly dawned on her that it was not anyone's fault that she felt so different from other people, and she began to turn back to a world that she had rejected. Her gradual acceptance of her environment, with all its loudness and brashness, allowed her, in turn, to feel more accepted. She became less vigilant, less ready for attack. Finally, she began to accept and value her sensitivity. She was able to appreciate the vivid, nuanced, vibrating world that her sensitivity revealed to her, and even to begin to describe it to others.

Letting Life Flow

During these same months of work, we continued to practice the exercise of attuning to fundamental consciousness. The most helpful part of the exercise for Eva was attuning to the stillness of the pervasive space and the movement of her breath at the same time. The breath passes through the stillness of fundamental consciousness without disturbing or altering it. This practice helped her to also experience how her thoughts, emotions, and physical sensations, even the sights and sounds in her environment, could move through the space without disrupting its stillness.

This exercise can help us distinguish the stillness of our true identity, the subtle ground of our being, from the movement of all our experience. This does not mean that we are separate from, or less affected by, our experience. Just the opposite: the more we identify with the stillness of fundamental consciousness, the more deeply we experience life. For as fundamental consciousness, we do not interfere with the flow of our thoughts, emotions, sensations, and perceptions.

Fundamental Consciousness and the Senses

I taught Eva the exercise of hearing and seeing as fundamental consciousness.

First, she attuned equally to the space pervading her body and environment, with her eyes open.

Then I said, "Experience that all of the sounds that you are hearing right now are occurring in the stillness of the space, without disturbing the stillness. The space itself is hearing the sounds. You do not have to listen in order to hear—you can receive the sounds without any effort. The sounds are vibrational patterns that pass through the space without changing it in any way."

Eva and I both sat in the openness of the space as the sound of the heater and of the distant traffic passed through it. Amazingly, one lone bird began to sing in that very moment, each note ringing like a bell in the open, unguarded silence of our hearing.

"Now," I continued, "allow everything that you see to just be in the space, just as it is. Your visual field relaxes and becomes one with fundamental consciousness. The space itself is doing the seeing—you do not have to look in order to see. You can receive the visual images without any effort."

Eva was able to let the space do the hearing, but seeing with fundamental consciousness was more difficult for her. I told her to look out the window at the windblown branches of the tree. "See if you can experience the stillness of the space and the leaves moving through the space without disturbing the stillness. It is the same as letting your breath pass through the space. The stillness and the movement are there at the same time."

As Eva gazed out the window, I was reminded of our first session, when she had sought refuge from our encounter among the trees outside. Now, she remained in her body and felt the space pervading herself and the trees at the same time. As I watched, she gradually loosened her visual grip, and the last bit of opaqueness in her eyes dissolved.

I went on, "Experience that everything you hear and everything you see occurs at the same time in the space without disturbing it. The sights and sounds emerge directly out of the space. You are seeing and hearing without any effort." For the first time since I'd known her, Eva seemed at ease.

She did not have to defend herself, and she was not pulled out of her body by the sights and sounds around her.

Eva found that this practice made it much easier for her to experience the transparency of herself and her environment in an ongoing way. She no longer had to attune to the space, but found herself there whenever she thought to focus on it. She began to have much more tolerance for abrasive sights and sounds. She could face the abstract painting in my office without feeling swirled around herself, and she could brave the heavy rhythms of the music at her health club without the exhaustion she once felt.

Still, Eva felt overwhelmed, or "displaced," by the vibrations of other people. She had begun to sit on the couch where my other clients sat, but if a particularly anguished person left my office before her session, she would not sit in that person's place, because she felt disturbed by that person's vibrations. Although she was often lonely, and had begun to talk about the possibility of finding a lover, she was afraid to attend social activities. Groups of people still made her feel "jumbled."

So we practiced another exercise to help her become more stable in the spiritual dimension, so that she could allow even human vibrations to pass through the clear space of her being.

Throwing the Pea

Sitting fairly close to her, I asked Eva to feel that the space that pervaded her body also pervaded me. By now she could do this quite easily, remaining in her own body as she rested in the space that pervaded us both.

I said to her, "I have an imaginary little red ball, about the size of a pea, and I'm going to toss it through the space over your right shoulder. I want you to let this ball pass through the space."

Eva laughed at this instruction. Since there was nothing over her shoulder and no actual red ball, it didn't sound like it would be too challenging. But when I actually pretended to toss the ball, she was surprised to find that she stopped its passage about mid-way over her shoulder.

Although there was no red ball, its passage was not entirely imaginary. The action of my toss—a flick of the wrist and hand—sent a current of energy through the space. This current was made more vivid by Eva's own image of the ball. The energy current from my hand collided with subtle holding patterns in the space of Eva's consciousness. These protective patterns are not just inside the body; they affect the space surrounding the body as well. Eva's long history of vigilance and protection from the world around her had created actual static densities in the space around her head. She was able to feel how these densities stopped the energy current from my hand. With a little concentration, she was able to release them so that on the second try the imagined ball went right through the space.

I proceeded to toss the imaginary ball through the space over her left shoulder, and then through her shoulders themselves, so that she could experience how vibrations from the environment even move through the transparency of the body without getting "caught" there or changing the space inside the body in any way.

Then I sat down next to her on the couch. This was a bit startling for Eva, but she managed to stay inside her body and open to the space that pervaded us both.

"Now I'm going to pretend to be crying," I said to her. "And I want you to let the sound of my crying pass right through the space, exactly as you let the imaginary ball pass through."

As I made the sound of crying, I felt Eva close off her attunement to fundamental consciousness, so that we were no longer in unified space. When I pointed this out to her, she was able to experience her protective movement. We tried again, and she found that she could remain open and allow the sound my grief to pass through the space.

Eva's pattern had been to protect herself against the vibrations of other people, creating a sense of alienation from the world around her. Some sensitive people do not protect themselves in this way, and simply surrender to an ongoing sense of overwhelm and merging with other people. On several occasions when I've taught this exercise, a client has begun to cry as soon as they hear the sound of my crying. Recently, a young woman began to cry as soon as I told her that I was going to pretend to cry, before I had even made the sound. This extreme emotional responsiveness is another type of spiritual openness that can also produce particular challenges and patterns of self-protection. I will address this in chapter 6.

In the following weeks, Eva practiced this new skill with other people in her life, in social settings, and at work. After a while, she found that she could allow the vibrations of other people to pass through her attunement to fundamental consciousness, in any situation. This meant that she did not have to be on guard against a potentially overwhelming encounter.

She also found that she was feeling more emotionally responsive toward other people, because she was not closing herself off to their experience. "I love people," she reported with some surprise. She could now feel an ongoing sense of warmth in her heart, and a kind of love that she had not even known about before. She described this love as welling up unexpectedly for specific people, and also for humanity as a whole, love that was "both distant and close at the same time." "And it's so amazing," she said to me. "People are made of the same stuff as trees!"

• • •

Sensory sensitivity, as we have seen, is a gift that can help us awaken to our spiritual essence. By becoming even more sensitive, we can uncover a subtle, unified dimension of ourselves in which stimuli register without overwhelming us. We can enjoy a world of vivid and subtle sights, sounds, fragrances, tastes, and textures. We can even sense an inner world beyond or beneath the surfaces of the life around us, the movement of thoughts and feelings in other people's bodies, and the subtle, multi-colored vibrations that emanate from all natural forms. To know someone with this gift is to be invited into this rich sensory world, even to have your own senses stretched open and receive some of this gift yourself.

EXERCISE 9 **Throwing the Pea**

This exercise is practiced by two people. Sit upright, facing each other about a foot apart, with your eyes open.

Feel that you are inside your whole body at once. Find the space outside of your body. Feel that the space inside and outside of your body is the same continuous space. Experience that the space that pervades your own body also pervades your partner's body. Do not move at all from within your own body as you attune to this pervasive space.

Partner A now tosses an imaginary red ball, about the size of a pea, through the space over Partner B's right shoulder. This is a gentle toss, but firm enough to send the ball all the way through the space. Partner B allows this ball to pass through the space, without stopping it or grasping on to it. This can take a little practice. Repeat two or three times and then go on to Partner A tossing the ball over Partner B's left shoulder.

Now Partner A tosses the imaginary ball gently through Partner B's right shoulder. Partner B allows the ball to pass through the space of his or her right shoulder. Even the body is made of empty space, so that the ball can go through without obstruction. Repeat with Partner A tossing the ball through Partner B's left shoulder.

Now Partner A stands next to Partner B and makes a sad or angry sound. Partner B allows this sound to pass through the space without either obstructing or grasping on to it.

Change roles, with Partner B tossing the ball, and Partner A allowing it to pass through the space.

This exercise can also be practiced without a partner. You can use sound to help cultivate and stabilize your openness to spiritual essence. Begin by practicing with a pleasant sound, such as music. See if you can allow the sound to pass through your body, and through your subtle consciousness, without feeling jolted or disrupted. When you can do this, you can try it with more abrasive sounds, such as the sound of traffic.

Walking down a city street, or in a crowded environment such as a grocery store, practice allowing all of the sounds, sights, and smells, as well as the vibrations of the people, to pass through the clear space that pervades your body and environment. Remember that your basic nature cannot be altered in any way by the stimuli in the environment.

Chapter 5

Landing on Earth: The Challenge of Grounding

DAVID HAD SILKY blonde hair down to his shoulders and a beatific smile that did not quite mask the sadness in his eyes. While he smiled at me in a somewhat distant benediction, I had the impression of a small boy looking out from his eyes with longing and despair. David had come to me because he felt at a crossroads in his life, unable to decide which direction to choose. He felt both bored and daunted by the need to make a living and to find a comfortable place in which to live. He wanted to go far away, to dedicate himself wholly to spiritual life, but he felt conflicted. Something seemed unfinished to him, and held him here in the ordinary world.

As he sat across from me and related this dilemma, I was aware of the tremendous light above his head. He was glowing, from his forehead upward. The bottom of his body, however, especially his pelvis, was tight and lifeless. I could feel the discomfort of this imbalance. He had no foundation, nothing to support the brilliant expanse at the top of his being.

I felt great respect for David, not just because of the light that emanated from the top of his head, but also because he knew that even with all that light, something was not quite right. He knew that he needed to heal. Even so, it was a struggle. As he talked, it was clear that he felt he had to convince me that he had no interest in the world, did not need a profession or friends or an intimate relationship. He viewed these things as distractions that kept other people from seeing the truth. He addressed me sometimes as his ally, someone who would validate his dedication to his spiritual path, and sometimes as his enemy, the conventional drudge who would condemn his life choices as weird or sick.

But I had no opinion about his life choices. I do not think it is any healthier to have a job and a family than to live as a hermit in the woods or on an ashram in India. I was only concerned with the openness of his being, the many contradictions and conflicts that dwelled in him, especially the deep fragmentation between his upper and lower body. I wanted to help David become open in his whole body, not because I thought he must have sexual intimacy in his life or a conventional job, but because I thought that his progression on his spiritual path depended on it. He needed to find his whole being so that he could uncover his whole light.

Personal History and Spiritual Transcendence

People who are spiritually gifted often have particularly strong wills. At the same time, they are also often extremely impressionable or malleable, as if they were actually made of a more porous material than most other people. This combination means that they can constrict themselves deeply and with great force. Because of this, they are often very open in some areas of themselves and very closed in others—they embody a wide range of maturity and immaturity. This was true of David, who was extremely open in his head and tightly closed in his pelvis.

After several meetings with David, I began to inquire about his childhood background, his relationship with his parents. In response, he offered me a well-considered psychological profile of each of them. His mother had been a talented painter but had given up her art to raise her three children. She had been brought up to value family life above all else and devoted herself completely to their care, but she often seemed worn out and somehow fragile, as if life were too much for her. Sometimes, David said, she would look lost or disoriented, as if she did not know how she had wound up in this situation.

David's father had also sacrificed himself for the sake of his family. He worked selling insurance, driving around all day to people's homes. When he was home, he only wanted to be left alone; he was tired of people. He sat in his favorite chair in the living room, drinking scotch and staring blindly into space. David's mother cautioned the children to stay away from him, to stay upstairs and be quiet, often assuring them of how much their father loved them, that he just needed to "mellow out." By the time David was ten, he knew that she was reassuring herself, that she also felt afraid to disturb the man downstairs.

Like most of David's conversation, these insights were expressed with little emotion. Although his words were compassionate, his tone was not. When I remarked on this, I became the enemy again, the spiritual ignoramus: didn't I see that this was just a story, that it had no relevance to David's true identity?

I shared with David my view that knowing our personal history can help us understand how we have organized ourselves, and how we have limited ourselves in order to cope with the world around us. Also, to remember ourselves throughout the various stages of our lives is to connect with the courage and intelligence with which we navigated our childhood environment and the challenges of adulthood. Knowing ourselves intimately and precisely, we may begin to regard ourselves with compassion and respect.

In the following weeks, I brought our conversation around again to the scenario he had described: the exhausted but intimidating presence of his father in the living room; the timid, lonely mother upstairs with the children. I wanted to know: did David ever misbehave? What happened if he was not quiet enough, if he did not give his father a wide enough berth?

As if reaching far down into some long forgotten part of himself, David, now with a forced casualness, said, "Then he beat me. But it wasn't often, just when he was really drunk."

"With a belt?" I asked.

"Yes, sure, with a belt. But it didn't hurt."

As he said this, the tightness in his pelvis increased, and his upward imbalance intensified. For a moment, I saw the little boy, clearly revealed.

"Where did he hit you?" I asked.

"Just on my butt," he said. "I really didn't feel anything."

David had managed to tighten his pelvis so thoroughly that he actually did not feel the pain of being beaten with a belt. He had also closed himself off to the humiliation and sorrow of this encounter with his father. By rising up to live mostly in the top of his head, he literally rose above the gritty, complicated horror of the situation.

By numbing himself to the physical impact of his father's belt, and to his father's anger and lack of caring, he had also numbed himself against the possibility of another person's anger and uncaring. Unconsciously, he had made himself unavailable to any human encounters that might repeat that painful rift with his father. As an adult, he had convinced himself that he simply did not exist in the realms of physical sensation and emotion in which other people seemed so comfortable. David's abundant capacity for love was not to be shared with the human world, except in the abstract, as unconditional love for humanity in general. From the lofty position above his head, David enjoyed a sense of expanded benevolence that was not subject to betrayal. But that small, sad boy still gazed out of his eyes. The loss of his father's love lived on his body.

"I want to float!" he told me.

"You will always be able to float," I said. "But now you float with only a small part of yourself, the top of your head. If you can inhabit your body as a whole, you will be able to float with your whole being."

It was a reflection of David's devotion to his spiritual path, wherever that might take him, and his desperation to be free of whatever was binding him, that he decided to give my methods a try. In the weeks that followed, we practiced the first Realization Process exercise of inhabiting the body. It was extremely difficult for him, but he applied the great strength of his will to persevere. He felt terrible sensations in his body. When he attempted to inhabit his pelvis, he said that he felt as if he were being "gripped by giant tweezers."

One day, as we made our way through the exercise again, he had a revelation. He suddenly realized that he was not being gripped; he was gripping himself. It wasn't tweezers at all. It was a little boy squeezing himself shut with all his strength. He could feel the defiance and the desperation in the child's mind, and the determination in the force of his muscles. Now he was able to grip his pelvis and let it go at will. Each time he let it go, it opened and softened a little more. Finally, he could feel the sting of his father's belt against his flesh, and he cried and cried. My whole office filled with his grief.

In the next session, David related that he felt fear walking down the streets of the city. He had always felt this fear but in the past he had managed to ignore it, to tune out other people and his own response to them. Now he was very aware of feeling that the other people he encountered were somehow stronger or more substantial than he was. It was not exactly a fear of being physically attacked, which he knew would probably not occur, but more of being somehow overpowered by their vitality.

Grounding Exercise

Although David had ample vitality in his own body, his upward displacement in the way he lived in his body made him feel weak, a "pushover." I worked with David to help him become more grounded.

I asked him to stand and to feel that he was inside his feet, that he inhabited them. The feet are a very effective foundation if we inhabit them completely, from the toes to the heels.

Then I instructed him to experience that there was no separation between him and the floor. He was able to feel this, but each time he inhaled, he lifted out of his feet and went back up to the top of his body. I asked him to let his breath adjust to him being in his feet. He had to find a different, whole body way of breathing in order to stay in his feet as he breathed.

I continued the exercise, asking David to inhabit his ankles and to feel the internal continuity between his ankles and his feet.

Then I asked him to feel that he inhabited his legs and then his pelvis, and to feel that he was standing *in* his legs, rather than on them.

David did not like the feeling of inhabiting his lower body. He said that he felt a great heaviness binding him to the ground.

"Can I walk like this?" he asked.

"Try," I suggested.

He took a few slow, hesitant steps across the floor of my office, and then stopped, looking surprised. "Well, I do feel stronger," he said.

Some experts on the body claim that human beings suffer from having made the evolutionary shift from getting about on all fours to standing upright on two feet. They suggest that standing is somehow not our "natural" position. This is not true; we would not have made the shift to two feet if we had not been ready to do so. As I explained in chapter 1, when we stand upright, we can receive an upward current of energy that comes up from the ground and moves through our body. This energy supports the body internally, making it buoyant and very easy to stand. This only happens if we inhabit our body, so that the body is open to receive the upward energy.

I asked David to find the centers of the bottom of his heels, and then to balance his awareness of these two points. Then I asked him to find the point just before the ball of each foot (the metatarsal), and to balance his awareness of those two points. Then I asked him to open these four points to receive the upward current of energy that came from below his feet and to receive it within his ankles.

I asked him to find the inside of his hip sockets and to balance his awareness of those two points. I encouraged him to receive the upward energy current in his hip sockets. As the exercise progressed, I asked him to receive the upward current in the center of his chest and shoulder sockets (from where it flowed down through his arms) and then within the center of his head, and finally to feel it passing up through the center of the top of his head—all the while still feeling connection to the origin of the current from below his feet. In order to receive this upward current of energy, we need to be settled toward the ground throughout the whole internal space of our body. Even the top of our head needs to be gently settled for the energy to pass through it.

With some practice, this energy flow coming up from the ground relieved the heaviness that David felt as he inhabited his feet and legs. He began to feel alive through his whole being.

The Qualities of Power and Gender

Wherever we inhabit our body, we can also feel the qualities of our being that emanate from those parts of our body. Likewise, if we attune to the qualities of our being, it helps us inhabit the corresponding parts of our body. Often, we avoid being in part of our body in order to avoid experiencing that particular quality of our being.

I worked with David to attune to the quality of his power within his midsection and the quality of his gender within his pelvis. David was very hesitant to feel the quality of power. He was afraid that if he felt power, he would become violent like his father. So we began by having him inhabit his chest and attune to the quality of love within his chest. David was relieved and comforted to feel that he had love in his chest. This was not love for any particular person. It was a part of his own being, a feeling that would always be there as part of his basic nature, even when he was alone. It was also a readiness to love others, a potential to respond to others from within the depth of his chest.

Then I asked him to inhabit the internal space of his midsection and his chest at the same time. Our body has space for both love and power at the same time. To feel both qualities at the same time enriches each of them. Secure in the presence of his love, David was able to attune to power in his midsection and let that support the love in his chest. When David felt this integration for the first time, he cried. He suddenly felt compassion for his father, who had not known how to feel this. "He would have wanted to," he said to me. "I know that he would have wanted to feel this."

Being with Other People

As David began to inhabit his whole body, he had to confront his fear and distrust of other people. His upward displacement in his body meant that he had always lived a little above other people. He didn't necessarily feel superior to them, only that he lived in a different realm where he didn't need to be concerned with them. He accepted the sense of isolation this gave him as necessary for his focus on spiritual life. For a certain phase of his spiritual practice, isolation may have been helpful. But since this isolation was the result of holding patterns in his body, to really let go of himself meant that he needed to dissolve his protective hermitage.

Since our spiritual dimension pervades our whole body, spiritual maturity is not a rising above our humanness, but rather the culmination of our humanness. It is not different than the ordinary human realm; it is our most subtle attunement to that realm. The spiritual dimension is right here, now, pervading everything. When we let go of our protective grip on ourselves, we land on the luminous, transparent earth.

One day, as I was leading David through the first Realization Process exercise, I noticed that his body was becoming increasingly integrated, but that there was still a fragmentation between his eyes and everything below his eyes. When we got to the part of the exercise where he was to inhabit his eyes, I asked him to let his eyes soften, so that they felt continuous with the rest of his face. Although he had heard this instruction many times before, this time he was able to really let go of his eyes, and in doing so, his whole body became even more deeply and fully unified. When he opened his eyes and looked at me, however, the fragmentation returned. I asked him if he could feel the same continuity between his eyes and the rest of his face with his eyes open. When he did this, for the first time there was a resonance of love between his body and mine. We were in the same space. By coming more fully into his body, there was a natural contact, and a spontaneous energetic flow between him and other people.

David had often spoken to me about wanting to get "beyond the ego." The word "ego" has many meanings, but the protective ego is protecting us primarily from other people, from repeating the hurts and humiliations that we suffered in our early relationships. When we arrive beyond the ego, we open to other people.

For most sensitive people, the main obstacle to opening to other people is the fear of being overwhelmed or annihilated by them. If we remain within our own body, we can receive them, and allow ourselves to be moved by them, without losing the fundamental stillness and presence of our true identity. We can be present and receptive at the same time.

When David had become adept at being both present in his body and open to other people, he no longer felt threatened or overpowered by them. He reported that he could feel connected to other people, without having to be like them.

For David, the most important benefit of being in his whole body was how it changed his spiritual experience. By inhabiting his body, he entered into a subtle dimension of himself that he had never known before. He described this as feeling that his whole body was made of light, the same light that he could feel above his head. Now he could also sense or even see this light in other people. He said that he had read about this for years, but had doubted it was even possible: that everyone and even every thing is made of the same spirit, the same spiritual light.

Strengthening the Inner Core

In the last section, we looked at the common problem, especially among people who are spiritually open, of living more in the top of the body than the bottom. There is another type of ungroundedness that is not an upward displacement. This is a pattern of diffusion or "spaciness." People who are diffuse have difficulty feeling centered in themselves. They feel, and look, somewhat hazy and unfocused, as though they are somehow dispersed outward into the space around them.

Laura came to me because at forty, she felt that she had not yet become who she wanted to be in either her work or her relationships. She was a writer who had published several poems in major magazines, and was now working, with some difficulty, on her first novel. She said that she always finished her poems in two or three weeks, but she was finding it much more challenging to maintain her focus on the larger project of the novel.

Laura had a fragile, ethereal quality. I found myself feeling maternal toward her, as if responding to a need for sustenance. But when we sat together, I felt that we were not quite connecting with each other. She smiled often and was polite and gracious, but still there was something lacking between us. In our conversations, she seemed to be speaking more to herself than to me. I experienced Laura's energy as a great cloud around her head, while the inside of her body seemed strangely blank or empty. This gave her a diffuse, diluted quality, as if she were not quite present in the room with me.

Laura was well aware of her difficulty with social contact. Her awkward attempts to relate with other people left her feeling defective and ashamed. She was glad to talk about her childhood with me, but she had been in therapy with several other therapists for many years, and had never found the key to relieving her discomfort. Over the course of several weeks, she described to me a large, relatively harmonious family. She was the middle child of seven siblings. Although she felt generally loved by all of her family members, she also often felt overlooked. She remembered spending a lot of time "in her own world," daydreaming. She had found that she could filter out the bustle and noise of her family and give herself over to reverie. She could remember being teased by her classmates at school but the presence of the other children was somehow muted in her memory, as if their voices could not quite reach her.

Now she still felt unreachable, but she also felt trapped in this state. She knew that she habitually muffled the world around her as she did in her childhood, but she did not know how to change that. She described it as feeling "spread out in the atmosphere." She also associated this diffuse feeling with her writing, her ability to set herself loose within her imagination and receive the words and images that became her poems. Just as David was afraid that he would lose his spiritual openness if he came down into his body, Laura was afraid that if she lost this diffuse quality, she would lose her creativity.

Laura understood that she had withdrawn from the hectic environment of her childhood home so that she could hear her own thoughts. She needed to create her own island within that environment so that her rich imagination would not be intruded upon by the hubbub surrounding her. She learned to be obedient and friendly so that no one would notice that she was not really there.

Laura also felt that as the middle child, she was excluded from the family alliances. Her younger siblings formed one unit, and her older siblings formed another unit, and she was somehow left without any close connections. She felt disconnected from her parents as well. They seemed to have no time to attend to anything but the most practical requirements of keeping the family fed, clean, and housed.

But it was more than that. Laura also felt somehow different from everyone in the family. She described it as being "made of a different fabric." When she did try to share her thoughts at the dinner table or during family events, she felt met by blank stares, as if she had not even spoken. The largeness of her family made her sense of aloneness even more acute. She concluded that she must be very odd to elicit such a lack of comprehension from so many people. It seemed that the only company that was really satisfying for her was her own.

Now, even to be present in the room with me for the duration of our hour sessions evoked her fear that she would lose her connection with herself or inadvertently reveal herself and be met with incomprehension. As she confided this to me, she realized that she was actually terrified to experience my incomprehension of her. It would feel as if I were destroying her.

As we explored this further, it became clear that her social fears affected her creative work as well. At first, Laura had thought that she was having difficulty working on her novel because of the concentration it demanded. She was surprised at this, since her poems, although completed in less time, also required hours of focused work at her computer. As she talked about it, she realized that it was not the concentration that was a problem for her, but rather the possibility that the book would be read by many people. Unlike her poems, which disappeared into obscure magazines, she imagined her book sitting conspicuously on the shelves of bookstores, maybe even reviewed in major publications and read by a wide audience. Although she knew that it was irrational, she felt terrified that these readers would invade her mental island and disturb her peace. In order to write her novel, she had to resolve her fear of being reached and seen by other people, and her dread of the various ways they might respond to her.

Laura had chosen to work with me because she knew that I had other ways of approaching psychological problems besides just talking. She was reluctant, however, to learn the Realization Process exercises. Anything "spiritual" frightened her. She had tried meditation only once before and had experienced a terrifying sense of disappearing into thin air as soon as she closed her eyes. "I really don't know where I went," she said to me. "But I know that I don't want to go there again."

People who have a lot of energy, like Laura, are sometimes able to "trance out" in meditation. By trance, I mean that they ride their energy upward or outward, away from their body, leaving the internal space of their body vacant. This experience, especially if it is unexpected and unexplained, can be alarming for the meditator. Trance states, in which practitioners attempt to vacate themselves in order, for example, to receive spirits or messages from the spirit world, are cultivated in some religious sects. This experience is very different than awakening to our unified, pervasive spiritual essence. In the Realization Process, we do not "go" anywhere. Rather, we are right here in a more conscious, subtle way. We feel present and embodied at the same time as we feel that we are made of empty space.

The Subtle Core of the Body

I began teaching Laura the Realization Process exercise of accessing and breathing within the subtle core of her body. As I described in chapter 2, this innermost channel is our entranceway into the all-pervasive space of fundamental consciousness. It is also our deepest contact with our individual being, and our deepest perspective on our environment. So it provides both distance from our environment and oneness with it at the same time. This means that we do not have to choose between connection with ourselves or connection with other people. For Laura, being able to live within her own core would mean that she no longer had to muffle the world in order to protect her connection to her own thoughts and creativity.

I began by asking Laura to close her eyes and find the center of her head. This point is in the center of the internal space of your head. It is not on your forehead, or on the top of your head; it is in the innermost depth of your head, between your ears. Like many people, Laura initially found a point above the center of her head. I asked her if she could come down a little within her head, until she felt an automatic resonance, or subtle vibration, down through her whole core, just by being in the center of her head. This was difficult for her. She said that she just felt "fuzziness" in the center of her head.

I taught her an exercise to help her access the internal space of her head. I asked her to draw an imaginary line starting at each ear and meet the two lines in the center of her head. As is also very common, she could more easily draw a line from one ear than the other. With a little practice, she was able to draw a line from each ear and meet the two lines in the center of her head. Then I asked her to hum across the line from ear to ear. Although she laughed at the silliness of this request, she tolerantly followed the instruction, humming across the imaginary line from ear to ear.

Now she was able to find the center of her head a little more clearly.

I continued, "Now initiate the breath within the center of your head, as if you had air within the center of your head that you could breathe."

Laura was surprised to actually feel some movement of her breath in the center of her head. "It's very subtle," she said.

"Yes," I agreed, "it begins as a very slight movement, but with practice you will be able to feel it more distinctly." She was also able to feel a faint resonance, or vibration, down through her whole vertical core as she breathed within the center of her head.

She then went on to try to initiate the breath within a point in the innermost core of her chest, and her pelvis, feeling the same vibration throughout her whole vertical core as she breathed within each center.

Laura had the most difficulty finding and breathing within the core of her chest. Instead of initiating the breath *within* the point, she was bringing her breath *to* the point. I stood next to her and put my fingertips on her back, just behind her chest center. I asked her to mentally find my hand. When she did this, I asked her to start her breath right there, where she was finding my hand, and to feel the breath move within that point even before she felt the breath move in her lungs. As Laura found that she could initiate the breath from this deep place in her chest, she began to sob.

"I don't know why I'm crying," she said. "I feel sad, but I also feel relieved. It's like I've been away, and now finally I'm back."

Breathing within the chest center can help release some of the sadness that we have held in our chests since childhood. Many people spontaneously use this metaphor of "coming home" to express the deep contact with themselves that occurs with this release.

When Laura was comfortable breathing from within each of the three points, I asked her to find all three at the same time. I then asked her to open her eyes and find all three centers again. "Usually we experience our environment from the surface of ourselves," I said. "See what it is like to experience the room from the core of yourself." Laura was surprised at how different this felt. "Everything seems further away, but somehow clearer, or crisper," she said. "But it's a little lonely."

Laura laughed when she heard herself say this, since she had just finished telling me about the lengths to which she had gone in order to be alone. Her words reflected a very important fact about our self-protective patterns. We create these patterns by freezing our energy and chronically tensing our muscles to create an actual barrier between ourselves and our environment, limiting the impact that events in our environment can have on us. Laura's pattern of diffusion, for example, was held in place by chronic tensions in her head and chest. The tensions of our protective patterns make it impossible to inhabit our body fully. Instead of living within ourselves, we live in the defensive barrier that we have created between ourselves and our environment. This limits our ability to connect with other people, and it also limits our ability to connect with ourselves.

Paradoxically, the barrier that is meant to protect us from the environment actually keeps us entangled with it.

This is because we always defend ourselves in relation to the outside world, so the defense is always a fixed, self/other pattern of energy. It holds and preserves the memory of our difficult relationship with our environment. Whether we withdraw inward, diffuse ourselves, block out, or push away the environment, that fixed energetic holding pattern keeps us in our old relationship with the environment that we are protecting ourselves against. Laura's pattern of diffusion held the memory of her boisterous family, even as it protected her from them. It both isolated her and kept her company.

To live in the subtle core of her body would mean to actually let go of her old relationship with her childhood environment. It would mean that she was really alone with herself, that her inner life of thoughts and feelings was really private. Laura was surprised to find herself crying at the thought of letting go of her family. "How will I survive without them?" she asked. Then she realized that she had been waiting, all this time, for them to finally accept her. She said, "If I let go of them, I will never get to be part of the family."

The Inward Ripening

Laura began to rapidly and visibly transform in the following weeks. Each time I saw her, she seemed more substantial, more focused. It was as if she were becoming alive deeper and deeper within her body. Instead of that diffuse, cloud-like quality, there was someone really there.

She also began, for the first time in her life, to value her difference from her siblings. "They don't really notice things the way I do," she said. "I guess that's why they never seemed interested in what I had to say." She had always felt "softer and slower" than the rest of her family. Now, she saw that these qualities that had made it so difficult for her to keep up with the verbal banter at the dinner table also allowed her a more subtle alertness to the world around her. With this recognition, she found that she could connect with her family members from the core of herself, without sacrificing her own way of being. She could allow her relationship with her family to be whatever it was in each encounter with them. As she began to accept that she might never be truly understood by her family, she also made more of an effort to cultivate friendships among her peers.

Over the year of our working together, she gradually became more comfortable in social situations, feeling that she could be both private within herself and connected to other people at the same time. She also allowed herself to withdraw from social situations when she felt "peopled out," accepting that she still sometimes preferred her own company.

I went on to teach Laura exercise 1 of the Realization Process (page 34): attuning to the space that pervaded her body and her environment as a unity. At first she was wary of "disappearing into space," as had happened in her previous meditation experience. But her ability to live in the core of herself helped her to experience the transparency of fundamental consciousness without vacating the internal space of her body. The space is presence itself, consciousness itself.

Laura also reported that her novel was progressing. She described how she could now open the whole space to her creativity. Rather than just receiving the words around her head, they seemed to well up through the empty listening presence of her whole being. She said that she often felt a mixture of strength and generosity as she expressed her personal, unique view of the world to whoever might want to read it.

EXERCISE 10 Couples Core-to-Core Attunement

With a partner, sit upright, facing each other, with your eyes open. Both partners follow the instructions at the same time.

Find the center of your head, between your ears, the very center of the internal space of your head. Now make eye contact with each other while remaining aware of the space between you. This awareness of the space between you while making eye contact may cause you to feel a little further away from your partner. This is your true distance. We often pull people closer to us or energetically merge with them through our eyes. We can also use our eyes to push people away.

Find the center of your head again. From the center of your head, find the center of your partner's head. Do not leave your own head to do this. You may feel a resonance between the center of your own head and the center of your partner's head.

From the center of your head, find your heart center in the center of your chest, deep in the core of your body. Now make eye contact while remaining aware of the space between you. Find your heart center again. From your heart center, find your partner's heart center. Be careful not to come out of your own heart center as you do this.

Find the center of your head again. From the center of your head, find your pelvic center, an inch or two below your navel, in the subtle core of your body. Now make eye contact while remaining aware of the space between you. Find your pelvic center again. From your own pelvic center, find your partner's pelvic center.

Now with all three points, find the center of your head again. Find the center of your head and your heart center at the same time. Find the center of your head, your heart center, and your pelvic center at the same time. Now make eye contact while remaining aware of the space between you. Find all three points in your own body again. From these three points, find the same three points in your partner's body.

This exercise can be done with any of the chakras, including the ones above your head.

EXERCISE 11 **Presence and Receptivity**

This exercise is practiced with a partner, with each person taking turns being the receiver.

Sit facing your partner. Begin by feeling that you inhabit your body; you are living within the internal space of your whole body at once. Let yourself experience your presence within your body. Staying within your body, allow yourself to receive the other person's presence within the internal space of your chest. Do not draw the person toward you, or push out toward them, but receive whatever vibrations or qualities emanate from him or her within your own chest. Now practice receiving the other person within your whole body.

When both partners have had a turn receiving the other person, then you can both practice receiving the other person at the same time. Stay present within your own body as you receive the other person.

This exercise can also be practiced on your own. Let yourself be present within your own body and receive the presence of the other people you encounter as you go about your daily life.

Chapter **6**

Hearing the Cries of the World: The Challenge of Being Happy

IN THE BUDDHIST tradition, a bodhisattva is said to be someone who hears the cries of the world. Extreme sensitivity to the emotions of other people, and the spontaneous upwelling of compassion in response to their suffering, is part of spiritual openness. It can ripen into the unconditional love and compassion of spiritual maturity.

Children with this type of openness have not yet developed the inner strength to withstand the emotional intensity that they feel around them. Nor do they possess the perspective to distinguish another person's emotions from their own. Their emotional sensitivity may even hamper their emotional development, for they may never find the inner peace or distance necessary to cultivate emotional resilience. Even as adults, they are shaken and pierced through by the emotions that course through their environment.

Children with this gift may also be confused by the contradiction between the emotional vibrations that they feel emanating from people's bodies and the verbal or facial expressions that deny these vibrations. This may cause them to become distrustful of themselves or others. Or they may become the confidant and/or the caretaker of the other family members. Their emotional depth and empathy make these children ideal receptacles for the family's sorrows.

They may also experience that their own emotional intensity is overwhelming for their parents. They often grow up seeing themselves as too emotional for anyone to bear. "I'm a terrible crybaby," they say of themselves, or "I'm fury on earth." They may attempt to clamp down on their emotional life or, conversely, to amplify their emotional responses as a desperate strategy to finally be heard.

As adults, these emotionally sensitive individuals often continue to suffer from their acute awareness of the pain around them. They ask, "How can I be content with my life, when so many people are unhappy?" Especially today, when our media brings the wars, famines, floods, and earthquakes from around the world into our living rooms, when we can probably each bring immediately to mind the image of a starving child, or of a mother crying over her son's body on a bombed-out street, any consideration for oneself may seem unforgivably petty and selfish. In this light, to mull over the slights of one's long-gone childhood, or to spend time dwelling meditatively in the depths of one's own being, may seem like the worst waste of time.

Yet, these deeply emotional souls do arrive in the therapist's office. Because they are attuned to the misfortunes of the world and aware of their own powerlessness to change them, life can become unbearable for them. They may also feel extremely lonely. It can be rare for them to meet someone who has the same depth of heart as themselves, so they often feel unmet in their relationships. If they do meet someone who can match them emotionally, it is sometimes difficult for them to experience a mutual exchange of feelings with that person. They may have been so habituated, since childhood, to being the givers of love and care, that they may not know how to receive them. They may also harbor a seemingly incongruous dependence on other people. If they adopted the parental role themselves in childhood, they may yearn to be truly mothered or fathered. They may be in desperate need of caretaking and comfort, even as they push them away.

Tolerating the Pain in the World

When Kathryn first came to work with me, she was full of apologies. She was sorry that she was a few minutes late for our first session, sorry that she had difficulty answering my question about why she had decided to begin this work, sorry that she had to pay me by check and not with cash, although I had expressed no preference for cash. She spoke quickly, in a soft, high-pitched voice, hardly pausing for breath. Her face was so expressive and shifted so rapidly from one emotion to another that I was reminded of the Beatles' lyric, "the girl with kaleidoscope eyes."

When I finally interrupted her to say that I was glad she had come, her monologue came to an abrupt stop. I smiled at her, and for an instant she sent me a flash of such pure sunlight that I felt a surge of warmth in my heart. Then, just as quickly, her expression changed to such extreme anguish that the whole room seemed to shift and darken. "I've been having trouble keeping it together," she almost whispered. She had folded so deeply into herself that I felt that I could barely reach her. "Please," I said, with more urgency than I knew I was feeling, "please tell me about it."

She began another unbroken string of sentences. Her father was very old and living alone, he needed her help but would never admit it, so that she had to beg him to let her visit, her cats were both ill, they needed to be given shots and fed with droppers at regular intervals, someone at work had just been diagnosed with breast cancer, the woman had two young children and no other means of support so Kathryn had offered to babysit for the children while the mother went for treatment, and there was an old woman who lived in her building that Kathryn visited most evenings, helping with dinner and cleaning the house, but lately the woman needed help bathing as well, the woman's own children hardly ever looked in on her and she could not afford professional help, and the news was so terrible, last week a whole family had burned to death in their home, had I heard about that? She knew that most people could filter it out but somehow she had never been able to do that.

As she spoke, Kathryn twisted and turned her thin body; she looked to me like a medieval woodcut of a person writhing in hell. When she finally ran out of words, we looked at each other for a long moment in the battered silence. Her pain was so deep that I felt my own tears forming.

"That's much too much for you to take care of," I said.

"I know, I know," she answered. "But my father, the woman at work, the old woman in my building, my cats, I'm all they have. But lately I'm so tired; I don't know what to do." Again we sat together silently. I had seen the flash of happiness in her smile, and I knew that that vibrant warmth was her potential, her gift, if she could allow herself to possess it.

Kathryn had never been to a therapist before and was not used to speaking about herself. She had not thought about her childhood for many years. Very gradually over the first months of our work together, she described to me the important events in her early life. Kathryn's mother had died when Kathryn was five. Her memories of her mother's illness, death, and funeral were vivid, and engaged all of her senses. She remembered her mother's face as cancer drained it of vitality, and the unfamiliar, frightening smell in her mother's sickroom. She could describe where the doctor and each of her family members were standing or sitting in the room the afternoon that her mother died, as well as what each of them was feeling: the grief, fear, resignation, and confusion that filled the atmosphere. She remembered wanting someone to hold her but looking around at everyone suffused in their own need and pain, and knowing that there was no one she could approach for comfort.

Kathryn had an older sister who, following their mother's death, turned her attention to practicing piano, shutting herself away in the music room for hours every day, and a younger brother who grew increasingly angry and remote. Her father was also withdrawn from the family, coming home from work exhausted and hiding himself away in his bedroom. His main communication with Kathryn was to ridicule her, portraying her to her siblings as a silly girl, and then, as she grew older and searched for ways to heal herself and her family members, as a "new age flake."

One of Kathryn's clearest memories of her childhood was of sitting at the kitchen table alone, listening to the different tones of distress in the house around her. She heard her sister's unhappiness in the timbre of the piano notes, her father's unabated grief in his footsteps above her, her brother's pain in the rejecting silence that issued from his room.

As an adult, Kathryn was still tuned in to the emotional pain in her environment. She felt it everywhere—at work, at the grocery store, in the subway—all of humanity seemed to be suffering. She was often more aware of what other people were feeling than what she was feeling. Her responsiveness to her environment obliterated her attunement to her own needs. Her emotions usually caught her by surprise, washing through her like tidal waves.

There was an upside of this for her. She could also feel overcome by joy. Describing a deer she had seen with its little fawn beside it, for example, brought blissful tears streaming down her face. Although Kathryn often found her emotional responsiveness painful, she enjoyed being "rocked to the core" with pleasure. She was a little wary that I might find a way to take this capacity away from her.

I have found that most sensitive people value their gifts, even when these gifts have caused them anguish or the derision of people close to them, and even when they have not been recognized or valued by others. Kathryn knew that her emotional responsiveness was something to be protected, even though it often made life intolerable for her. I assured her that she would not lose any of her emotional depth, nor would she become dispassionate toward the suffering that she encountered around her. Rather, by uncovering the stable, spiritual ground of her being, she would be able to tolerate, or encompass, her emotional responses. The more we know ourselves as the stillness of fundamental consciousness, the more deeply we can allow our emotions to move through this stillness, without feeling overwhelmed by them.

Developing Emotional Tolerance

I began by teaching Kathryn the exercise of inhabiting her body. She was able to do the exercise easily, but after several months, it became clear that she was not maintaining this inward attunement to herself. Even when we practiced the exercise during our sessions, I had the sense that she was doing it for me rather than for herself. She inhabited each part of her body dutifully, often opening her eyes to gauge my expression as I watched her. If I nodded encouragingly, she would close her eyes again and continue with the exercise.

Whenever I questioned her about how she experienced the exercise, she always replied that she felt very happy and peaceful while inhabiting her body. Although most people do feel a greater sense of contentment and calm when they embody themselves, many must initially confront more negative feelings that get in the way of this self-contact. Some feel, for example, that it would be dangerous to be fully present in their body, that this would make them too conspicuous, or that the sense of self-possession and individuality derived from embodiment would break some family taboo.

When I told Kathryn this, she acknowledged that although she felt fine doing the exercise with me, she did not want to attempt it in public. She said that she did not know the reason for her hesitance. I had the sense, however, that she did know but was reluctant to tell me. I asked her to imagine being in a public place or out with friends and inhabiting her body. She was unable to do this, and instead became even more constricted. Finally, she looked at me apologetically and said, "I know that this is crazy." "Yes?" I asked. Practically bent double, and so softly that I could barely hear her, she said, "It's just that I'm so powerful. I don't want people to be afraid of me."

This was Kathryn's dilemma. Once broached, she was able to confide her long history of feeling older, wiser, and somehow more powerful than other people, especially the people in her family, but needing to keep this knowledge hidden. She now saw how she had played her assigned role as the lowest, craziest member of the family, while squashing her secret knowledge of herself down into a tiny ball in the pit of her stomach. Attuning carefully to the memories of her interactions with her father, she could sense the small release of tension that he felt as he derided her, as well as her willing sacrifice of her own self-respect for this brief alleviation of his pain. If she inhabited her whole body, her secret would be out. She would lose her assigned place in the scheme of things, and she would be alone, cast out. And her family, how would they survive without this outlet for their misery?

Kathryn would have to relinquish her role in her family in order to claim her true abilities. For Kathryn, this felt like an acceptance of failure, the failure to relieve her father and siblings of their pain. She also feared that her father might be right. Maybe she was a flakey, silly girl, and her hidden belief in her own value was just a delusion to make herself feel better.

Many psychotherapists would interpret Kathryn's idea of her overwhelming power as a compensation for her feelings of shame and inferiority in her childhood home, and even her compulsion to help other people as a way of feeling more important. They would view the work with Kathryn as helping her accept herself as an ordinary human being.

I agree with this view, in part. I felt that Kathryn had held onto and even exaggerated the idea of her secret power as a protection against her family's assaults on her self-respect. It was also true that she possessed unusual emotional depth and sensitivity, and that none of the adults in her childhood had been able to recognize or to match this. I felt that her response to the suffering of others was genuine, and that the sense of responsibility she felt toward them was an impulse that came from that genuine response. I saw my work with her not so much as helping her to accept herself as ordinary, but to accept herself as gifted—to know herself as a gifted human being, rather than as either a superhuman or subhuman oddity. If she could acknowledge her gifts openly, to herself and others, then she would not need to protect them or exaggerate or apologize for them. She also needed to be able to tolerate the intensity of her emotional responses so that they did not overwhelm her attunement to her own needs and limits.

The Feel of Being Human

As Kathryn found the courage to inhabit her body, her fear of her own out-sized power was gradually replaced by the felt experience of the richness of her being. She said that she could feel how her intensity was as much inward as outward, so it would not be overpowering to other people. "It feels gentle and powerful at the same time," she said. One day as she was completing the exercise and inhabiting her whole body at once, she said, "I think I can really help people more if I'm in myself like this." "I think so, too," I agreed. Living within our body means that we are always connected to the spontaneous source of our love and compassion.

This contact with herself also helped Kathryn to experience her limitations, to feel when people were needing or asking for more than she could give. As she allowed herself to value her emotional gifts, she began to use them with more awareness and with more kindness toward herself. In the following months, she discovered that she was actually quite outgoing, that she enjoyed the company of other people, and that they usually welcomed her passionate nature. Her emotional depth did not set her apart from other people as she had feared. It contributed to her pleasure in connecting with them.

Letting Emotion Flow Through the Stillness of Fundamental Consciousness

Kathryn continued to practice the exercise of inhabiting her body and attuning to the clear space of fundamental consciousness pervading her body and everything around her. Gradually, she was able to distinguish the movement of her emotions from this ground of stillness. She could then feel that her emotions passed through her, as intense but transitory states. This meant that she was no longer overwhelmed by her emotional responses. She could remain present as they flared up and subsided within her body.

When we know ourselves as fundamental consciousness, we are also able to distinguish clearly between the movement of emotion in another person's body and the movement of emotion in our own body. This means that although we may respond emotionally to another person's anguish, we do not mistake it for our own. In the language of spiritual or psychic healers, we can experience other people's suffering without "taking it on." We can read another person's emotions without mirroring them in our own body.

The Acceptance of Suffering

One of the biggest challenges for Kathryn was to allow herself to feel content. Whenever she would begin to relax and enjoy life, she felt guilty. Kathryn recognized this feeling from her childhood: she would begin to feel happy, and then feel guilty because the rest of her family was in so much pain. As an adult, her attunement to the suffering of other people seemed to confirm her conclusion that feeling happy was selfish. One day when she was struggling with this, I told her that the first noble truth in Buddhism is that life is suffering. Kathryn was not familiar with Buddhism, and she was shocked that it would teach such a thing. "Do you believe that?" she asked.

"I believe that our basic nature is pure joy, and that the more open we become, the more we can feel that," I said. "But being open means letting go of our grip on ourselves. And part of letting go of ourselves is accepting life, just as it is. That means accepting that there will probably always be loss and anger and fear in the world, and in ourselves."

"You mean not to try to make things better?"

"No, I think it's good to try to help people as much as we can. But we also need to accept the suffering around us, and our own suffering as well. We need to encompass suffering in our love for the world."

Kathryn was quiet for a long time. Then she said, "I think that I have been angry at life for being so hard. I've probably been angry at God ever since my mother died. But I know it's true, everyone suffers, and everyone dies, no matter how much someone loves them or needs them. I guess I can sit with this for a while—accepting the suffering, so that I can also accept the happiness."

Becoming One's Own Caretaker

Felicia wrapped me in a warm embrace the moment she walked through the door for her first appointment. She was soft and round, with bright red curly hair and shining blue eyes. She sat comfortably on the couch with a reassuring, expansive expression. Once we were sitting face-to-face, though, I realized she was slightly unfocused and diffuse. She seemed to project herself toward me, as if trying to connect by merging with me. I was also aware of a heaviness in her chest, as if she were burdened by the weight of her lungs.

Like Kathryn, Felicia also described her reason for beginning therapy as her inability to take care of all the people who needed her. As we spoke, it became clear that she was furious about it, that she felt acutely the one-sidedness of her relationships with other people.

Even though her initial conversation was about her disappointment with so many people, Felicia was ready to put me in the role of savior. She had read my books, been

to my website; she knew that I could help her. I felt that
this idealization of me reflected her need to find someone
to care for her who would not need help themselves, someone—finally—whom she did not have to worry about. Still,
as we spoke, she searched my eyes and body, as if looking for
signs that I might be weakening beneath the onslaught of
her troubles.

Felicia described her desperation, as a small child, to
care for and cure her severely depressed mother. Often when
Felicia got home from school, her mother would be in bed,
the curtains of the room closed. Felicia would bring her
mother snacks from the kitchen, so that she could spend
some time with her. She also made her little figures out of
papier-mâché that sometimes brought a rare smile to her
mother's face.

Felicia was bitterly angry at her father for leaving her
mother for another woman and creating a new family
when Felicia was seventeen. She was also angry at her
older sister who rarely visited their mother, now living
in a nursing home, while Felicia visited several times a
week. When she told me about this, she sat forward on
the couch, leaning as far toward me as she could, her face
contorted with rage. "People don't care," she yelled at me.
"What's wrong with them?"

Throughout her whole childhood, Felicia served as
her mother's confidant and emotional support. Her father
had barely hidden affairs; her sister spent most of her time
smoking pot with friends in her room, and left home at

sixteen. None of the family's problems were ever spoken of. Her mother's depression, her father's philandering, her sister's drug use were all denied. "I was the only one who had a clue of what was going on," she said.

Felicia had always felt that she was on her own. With me, however, she expressed a childlike dependence, wanting me to advise her on decisions both big and small, and to comfort her for the slights and "cold shoulders" that she experienced almost daily in her interactions with other people. I felt my own heart stretched open by her urgent need to be held there, and by my attempt to meet her unflinchingly as she jabbed and roared at the world around her.

Felicia found her life so compelling emotionally that she never had the chance to live anywhere else in herself. She inhabited a whirlwind of feelings that gave her no rest. But psychological healing requires the ability to reflect on your situation, to see the big picture and make your peace with it. It requires balancing emotion with awareness. This awareness can be gained, in part, simply by talking about the circumstances that have caused you pain. Felicia and I spent many sessions looking at the events that had made her so angry and sad, so needing of support and yet unable to find it. Very gradually, she began to develop some perspective; she was able to look at these early situations and relationships, and make sense of how they had affected her.

Balancing Emotion with Awareness and Physical Sensation

I taught Felicia the exercise for balancing her emotional depth with awareness and physical sensation (described in chapter 2, page 46). I began by teaching her how to inhabit her body and attune to fundamental consciousness pervading her body and environment. I then asked her to attune to the quality of awareness in and around and above her head. This was unfamiliar territory for her. I stood next to her and placed my hand a few feet above her head. I asked her to mentally "find" my hand. She was then able to bring her attention to the space above her head. Just by finding this space above and around her head meant that she could experience the subtle quality of awareness. The reason for this is that the qualities are already there. We do not have to create them or imagine them.

"Now experience this quality of awareness pervading your whole body, as if you were completely made of this quality." Felicia held herself very still as she experienced this for the first time. Her body took on a lightness and clarity that I had never seen in her before. Her red curls glowed around her head.

"Now feel that the quality of awareness pervades you and your environment at the same time." Felicia was surprised at how different this felt from her usual way of experiencing herself and the world around her. "It's like a different climate," she said, "very bright and crisp. It must be autumn," she joked.

"Now attune to the quality of emotion," I continued. Automatically, Felicia brought her attention to her chest and midsection. She did this easily; it was her home ground. "Feel that your whole body is made of this emotional quality."

As Felicia did this, the anger and grief that had weighed heavily in her heart began to dissipate. Instead, the deep well of love that was her spiritual gift spread its subtle warmth throughout her whole body. I was so moved to find myself sitting with this beautiful buddha, made of love, that it was difficult for me to say the next line of instruction. "Now feel that this quality of emotion pervades your body and environment at the same time," I managed.

"Now attune to the quality of physical sensation. For this, you need to bring your attention way down to the space below your torso and your feet."

Felicia found that she could do this, even though she had never before felt the ground of physical sensation. Like most people, she had only felt specific sensations such as heat or touch. Physical sensation, though, is as much an aspect of the spiritual ground of our being, and of our oneness with everything around us, as awareness and emotion. She could easily feel that her whole body was made of physical sensation, but it was a new experience for her to feel physical sensation pervading her body and environment at the same time. "It's like everything is somehow made of touch," she said.

The exercise ends with attuning to all three qualities at the same time. First Felicia attuned to awareness and physical sensation at the same time, pervading her body and environment.

Then she "blended in" the quality of emotion pervading her whole body and environment. When we attune to all three qualities at the same time, they become indistinguishable from each other. They become the vibrant emptiness and quality-rich presence of fundamental consciousness.

With practice, Felicia's response to life became more balanced. Her emotions were just part of her experience, rather than her primary focus. She said that this seemed to "slow down" the way events in her life affected her, so that she had more understanding of what was happening. She still found her relationships with other people frustrating and confusing. "I am so hungry for something," she said, "but I don't seem to be able to get it."

This deep hunger for connection is often felt by spiritually sensitive people. It is sometimes expressed as a hunger for the divine. It comes, I believe, from an intuition of the oneness that we can feel with all other life, even with the cosmos. To know ourselves as the one, unified luminous ground, pervading everywhere and filling everything, finally satisfies this underlying sense of separation.

Relating in Fundamental Consciousness

I began to focus our sessions on the practice of attuning to fundamental consciousness pervading her body and environment at the same time. This was difficult for her to feel. Like many people who are very fluid and expansive energetically, she could easily leave her body and extend herself into the room. This had been her way of relating to other people all her life. She merged with them rather than actually experiencing the contact of her own being and another person's. This merging with others is an energetic movement outward. It means leaving oneself and entering into another person. Felicia knew that many people found her invasive, but she had never known how to change this way of relating. It felt to her as if other people were not available to her, or that her need for contact was too much for them.

Attunement to the stillness that pervades everywhere is a more subtle level of experience than extending oneself outward with one's energy. Rather than an outward movement, it feels as if we are settling into the space that is already there, without any effort on our part. In fact, we can only find this pervasive space by settling more deeply within our own body. Once we have found this space, we can stay in our own body, connected to our own being, while we experience contact with another person.

I began by asking Felicia to feel that the space pervaded us both, as I stood to the side of her so that she was not looking at me directly. When she was able to do this without leaving her body, I made the exercise more challenging by sitting in front of her.

Felicia found it very difficult to remain in her body with me sitting directly in front of her. She inhabited her body but still seemed to spill out toward me from the front of her chest. I suggested that she experience having a front to the container of her body. She could be inside the container of her body, and the container had a front to it so that she did not have to spill out of it.

Felicia tried this out, and suddenly looked at me with delight.

"I feel it", she said. "You're over there and I'm over here, but we're continuous with each other. I always thought that I had to either have armor separating me from people, or mix with them completely."

A look of amazement came over her face and she said, "I don't exist in space. I am space." This was an important insight and showed that she was actually realizing fundamental consciousness. This space is not something separate from ourselves. There is no difference between the space and our own self.

Felicia could now attune to the space pervading both of us, but only if she did not make eye contact with me. As soon as she tried to make eye contact with me, she came forward to merge with me. I said, "See if you can make eye contact with me across the distance between us. Be aware of the space between us as you contact me."

People often "glom onto" the world with their eyes, so that everything seems to be right on top of them. Being aware of the space between yourself and other people or things can give you more sense of the true distance between yourself and the world around you.

The first time Felicia was able to feel this, she laughed. "You look so much smaller," she said. As Felicia began to see me across the distance between us, as a person separate from herself, she seemed both less worried about me and less idealizing of me. At times, I thought I saw an expression of patience in her eyes as she regarded me, as if she were coming to terms with the flaws or vulnerabilities that she saw in me. I was no savior, but I was also not an enemy.

Fundamental consciousness is the basis of our universal kinship and equality with all other life. As Felicia and I continued to sit with each other as this unified, pervasive space, our contrived relationship of teacher and student (or doctor and patient) became secondary. We had a felt sense that we were made of the same essence, the same transparency. Although we each had our own history and perspective to communicate to each other, this could now take place in a context of ongoing contact between us. As fundamental consciousness, we knew, felt, and touched each other across the distance between us.

EXERCISE 12 **Intimacy and Space**

Sit in a public place, like a library or a park. Feel that you are inside your whole body at once. Find the space outside of your body. Experience that the space inside and outside of your body is the same, continuous space. You are in your body, but you are permeable, transparent. Let yourself feel that the space that pervades you also pervades the other people in the environment. Do not move at all from you own body as you experience this. Feel that there is no difference between you and the pervasive space; you *are* the space.

From the internal space of your own body, let yourself experience the internal space of the people around you. See if you can feel the life within their bodies and the particular qualities of their being. Stay in your own body as you experience this.

Attune to the quality of your awareness around and above your head. Experience the quality of awareness pervading your whole body. Experience the quality of awareness pervading you and the other people in the environment. Let the field of awareness pervade and receive you and the other people. Repeat this with the quality of emotion, then with the quality of physical sensation, and then with all three at once. Remember that when you attune to all three qualities at once, they become undifferentiated from each other. They become the quality-rich field of fundamental consciousness pervading you and the people around you.

Chapter 7

Shape Shifters: The Challenge of Being Authentic

CARLOS CASTANEDA WAS one of the mostly widely read writers in the early days of the American spiritual renaissance. For many of us, Castaneda's teacher, the Native American shaman Don Juan, was our first image of what it means to be a spiritual master. So, although I could no longer tell you the names of Castaneda's many books, I can remember vividly the description of Don Juan helping Castaneda to transform himself into a bird.[1]

The extreme development of the imagination is one of the traditional signposts of advanced spiritual maturity. Many shamanistic religions purport to having adepts who can transform themselves into animals. Both Tibetan Buddhist and Jewish folklore speak of great mystics who could create elaborate feasts or even humanoid creatures (such as *golems* in Judaism) by the power of their inner vision. Many Hindu masters have been said to be able to create a fragrance or even a bit of jewelry or a religious statue simply by imagining it. In the West, probably the most famous of these feats of creative imagination is the story of Christ transforming water into wine at a wedding.

The potential for this aspect of spiritual maturity is often present in spiritually gifted children as a rich capacity for imagination. Like all talents, it can cause difficulties. These dreamy, "woolgathering" children may find themselves distracted from the mundane pursuits of their peers. They may have difficulty concentrating on school work that bores them, when they can easily escape into more entertaining fantasies. With their "heads in the clouds," they may be ridiculed or ostracized by friends and family back on earth. These children may use their capacity for fantasy to avoid contact with the abrasive realities of their childhood environment, or to cope with their sense of alienation. They may also create false personae that are, because of the children's depth and sensitivity, both deeply distorting, and as they get older, extremely troubling for them.

Everyone grows up to be, to some extent, an abstraction, an idea of themselves, rather than the embodied, lived experience of themselves. We may identify ourselves with our role, such as teacher, or lawyer, or with an aspect of our personality, such as whiz kid, or victim. We construct personalities, such as a persona of graciousness or of intimidation, in order to cope with challenging social situations. We also pattern our constructed personalities on the personae of our parents or on the images of people in the media in order to appear more sexy or powerful.

As children we adjust ourselves in order to conform to the images that people project onto us. We may form ourselves into an image of cuteness, or naughtiness, or goodness, if our parents seem to see us like that or want us to be that way. If we observe children closely, we will see that the false smile, for example, can appear very early in life. Sensitive children may be particularly flexible or impressionable, and attuned to the way their parents want or need them to be. They may become quite lost in their attempt to evoke their parents' affection, contact, or approval.

Like our defensive patterns, some of these personality constructions become bound in the tissues of our bodies—they become part of the actual shapes of ourselves. Other patterns are more fluid; they are mannerisms or postures that we assume, usually unconsciously, in response to particular situations. All of these patterns mask and constrict our authentic self. They obstruct both our true reception of life (such as our ability to really see, hear, or touch) and our expression of ourselves—our ability, for example, to speak from our hearts.

In people with a high degree of imagination, the constructed personality is sometimes a more unusual façade than most people create. It may, for example, be the product and expression of an extreme sense of alienation from the world around them. It may also be a more thorough transformation of themselves. Because of their inward depth and the power of their will, they may be able to imprint a false image deeply within themselves and appear more askew from reality than the typical persona. Once, in India, I read a text that said that spiritual people disguise themselves in the world as madmen, ghouls, and children. Unfortunately, although our disguises may offer some protection from the world, they also hide our true nature from ourselves.

For spiritually sensitive people, their false personae may be a source of extreme discomfort. Because we form our personae unconsciously, most people are not aware that they are anything other than authentic. But spiritually gifted individuals may have a heightened intuition of reality, a particular ability to distinguish truth from artifice. Very often, their own dissonance grates on them. This, I think, is a type of suffering that is the particular province of the spiritually gifted: to feel trapped in one's own unreality.

Some people can, to some extent, drop their façade, or at least feel less encumbered by it, when they are alone. They may seek solitude because it is the only time when they feel real. Their inability to experience authenticity in the world with other people may become a great burden. They feel unable to reach the actuality of contact with themselves and others that they somehow know is possible, and that they yearn for. They cannot experience this authenticity unless they can recognize and see through their imagined self. The spiritual path, for everyone, but especially for people with exceptional imagination, involves distinguishing truth from fantasy. It is waking up from a dream.

Uncovering Reality

When I first met Shana, she was dressed elaborately in rich textures, abundant jewelry, and dramatic make-up that accentuated her large dark eyes. Her hair was dyed an opaque black and decorated with rhinestones. It was her manner that was most striking. She presented herself as if she were blessing me with her presence. As she spoke, she seemed to imbue herself with a supernatural glow.

She began by informing me that she knew for certain that she was not of this world. Her spirit had come from a distant part of the firmament in order to help heal and awaken the people of this planet. This assertion was illustrated by a celestial smile and outstretched arms. Although her smile and gesture seemed off-key to me, she somehow conveyed a sincere wish to make things better here. Even though I felt more like a spectator than a participant in our encounter, I found myself warming to her.

Much has been written and speculated about the relationship of severe mental illness and spiritual openness. It may be that spiritually gifted people, because of their fluidity and openness, are susceptible to mental illness, as they are susceptible to the other difficulties that I describe in this book. Mature spiritual realization is different from mental illness. It is a state of deepened contact with oneself and one's environment, without fragmentation or dissociation. Even though Shana had difficulty with contact, she did not fit the psychology field's criteria for psychosis. She had no hallucinations, no lack of coherence in her speech or thought, and no distortions of reference (thinking, for example, that ads on TV were talking about her). Although very fancily and creatively dressed, her presentation was not so odd as to raise alarm bells. Even her idea of being a "star person" was not that unusual; it is one of the beliefs that is taught and written about in the mystical reaches of our culture. I was also interested and reassured to see a kind of no-nonsense irritation in her movements and facial expression as one of the sub-strata beneath her fixed expression of benevolence.

Shana had come to me because she was at a crossroads in her professional life. She had worked for many years as a salesperson in a jewelry store, but she had aspirations to set up her own business as a psychic reader. She related several stories of her amazing ability to predict future events for her friends. She had even predicted the exact date that a woman would meet her future husband, as well as his physical attributes and profession, and was surprised herself when this came to pass exactly as she had seen it in the space around the woman's head. She had recently attended their wedding.

"I have magical powers," she informed me, with a mixture of pride and puzzlement. Yet she felt that something was stopping her from going ahead with her business plans. She knew that she was meant to take this next step in her life, and hoped that I could help her identify what was getting in her way.

Throughout our conversations, I was most aware of her inability or reluctance to make eye contact with me. Although she treated me with the slight disdain that a higher being has for a lower one, if I tried to look directly into her eyes, she reflexively turned away. In that quick gesture, I was able to glimpse the vulnerable, extremely sensitive woman who sat before me.

Exploring what it meant for her to reveal her powers to the world, she began to describe a childhood filled with confusion and rejection. She was surprised to find herself moved to tears by some of these memories. She thought that she had put all of that behind her. When she was in her early twenties, she had come across a book about aliens who had come to Earth as guides and healers, and she had realized that she must be one of them. Since that time she had never thought about her childhood, seeing it simply as an illusion, a kind of "cover story" to help her pass as human. She laughed a little as she told me this. It was clear that she did not entirely believe it; it just seemed like one possible explanation for her intense feeling of difference from other people.

"I've always felt out of kilter," she said, with a sudden bolt of honesty. "I know something is not quite right with me, but everything around me also seems out of kilter, so it's hard to get oriented. Does that make sense?" It seemed a strange complaint to her; she had never made it out loud before. She felt out of kilter in an out-of-kilter world. "There is so much contrivance, everywhere," she said.

It was several months before Shana came to trust me, and trust herself, enough to see through to what was really holding her back. When she told me about it, she covered her face with her hands as if to hide from me. "Maybe I'm a fraud," she said. I knew it was the worst thing she could think about herself. Then she lifted her head and for the first time looked me right in the eyes. "But I can really do those things I told you about." Then she looked away. "Am I just afraid that people will think I'm a fraud?" she asked herself. She was quiet for a long moment. "No, it's a feeling I have about myself, that I can't be real." She looked at me in wonder, as if it were the oddest thing that had ever occurred to her.

She said, "There's a Hindu prayer that says 'please lead me from illusion to reality.' I understand that prayer. That reality is what I want most of all."

Although Shana had understood her predicament clearly, she did not know how to reach the reality she wanted. She had many fears about seeing through the persona that she had created. She was also terrified that I would try to make her into something that she was not; some generic sample of a "normal" person.

She admitted to me that the world often seemed dull to her. Most people seemed narrow and boring, and those who didn't frightened her or seemed inaccessible. She could not find her place in the world, could not feel at ease. She passed through the various environments of her life as an exalted observer, perched on her own mountaintop. "I really am different from them," she told me. "In fact," she said defiantly, but with a humorous gleam in her eyes, "I am most like those star people. They are working for the good here. We are a network of advanced souls, working for the good." Now tears were streaming down her face. "I don't know why I'm crying," she said. "I want to be 'in the world but not of it,' but I also want to really be here, I want to be here with you."

Transforming Back Again

I remembered my own drop into reality. Before I began my spiritual practice, I lived in a world of vibration and imagination. As a dancer and choreographer from my childhood through my early twenties, I regarded life almost entirely as a dance. It was a dynamic display of moving textures, energies, and symbolic meanings. This display was a constant source of inspiration for me; it was easily translated into choreography.

I was enthralled by the meanings and drama that I saw or superimposed on the world around me. I was also disoriented. Although I had some connection to my body through my years of rigorous dance training, I did not inhabit my body. Especially as I became more technically proficient, my body seemed more like an object to me, something separate from myself, that I had crafted and honed to perform athletic feats. I mostly resided in a narrow band of myself above my eyes; not in my intellect, but in my imagination. When I injured my back and had to leave the cloistered dancer's world that had been my home, I too felt like an alien creature that had just landed on Earth.

After I underwent back surgery, I lived in a full-torso brace for six months, and my body relaxed. I began to meditate and to slowly settle within my body. I remember very well the tremendous sense of sobriety that fell on me at the beginning of this transition. Everything I looked at seemed to be starkly itself, stripped of symbolic value. The Tibetan Buddhist teacher Chögyam Trungpa called this the "rawness" of life. A tree was exactly a tree. It no longer became a metaphor for something else, like celebration, or reaching upward, as it would have when I was a dancer. It was just a tree. It was that very particular unique tree, but just a tree. I also felt strangely substantial, as if I suddenly had weight and volume. More than that, I felt ordinary, a person. It was as if the energies that I had sent out into the great beyond had now returned and settled inward, within my skin. I was just me.

So I felt that I understood Shana's fears. To become real, to be embodied, meant a kind of surrender to materiality. We cannot know ahead of this surrender, this letting go of our fantasized life, that real life is materiality suffused with energy and consciousness; it is both solidity and radiant transparency. It is both the most ordinary, sober experience of ourselves and our environment, and the most extraordinary, at the same time. We also cannot know before this letting go that our imagination is not extinguished with spiritual awakening; it matures.

The Reality of the Body

The shift from living in one's imagination to living in reality is not just a mental transition. It is a change in the way we inhabit our body. In our first session, when Shana held out her arms to express her mission to heal the world, the reason that it did not seem authentic to me was that she was not really in her arms. There was a lack of connection between her being and her body that kept her from truly expressing herself to other people.

The reality of actual contact with oneself is, at the same time, actual contact with our environment. It is a very interesting aspect of our nature that to heal the split between body and mind is, at the same time, to heal the split between oneself and one's surroundings, or between oneself and other people. Life is, to some extent, imaginary or illusory—for everyone. We all regard life through the filter of our past experience and our templates, our early learning of the world. We all color our circumstances with our hopes and fears. We also imagine a barrier between ourselves and our environment. We imagine a separation between a world out there and the consciousness (in here) that perceives that world.

As we come into greater contact with ourselves and the world, these filters and projections begin to dissolve. We find that there is no separation between ourselves as subject and what we perceive as object. All of our experience, both internal and external, registers at once in the same single, unified expanse of consciousness. This direct, immediate contact with life feels like it is happening right now; it feels real; it feels complete; there is no part of ourselves that is left out of the experience of the present moment.

The reality that the Hindu prayer pleads for is not the world most people perceive of separate, solid material objects. The sobriety of spiritual practice is a stripping down, not to matter, but to something much more mysterious, to the unified luminous transparency pervading everything. We cannot get to this dimension by avoiding the material world. We need to accept and penetrate through the world of separate solid objects, and to inhabit fully our own separate physical body in order to experience ourselves and our environment as the single expanse of fundamental consciousness.

When we live within our body, we find the center of our own being, and of all being. In reality, we all share this same one center. When we live in our imaginations, we are off-center. Interestingly, human beings have the capacity to discern balance from imbalance, center from off-center. This capacity allows us, for example, to distinguish harmony from dissonance in both sound and visual forms.

This type of attunement is particularly acute in people who are spiritually open. Shana was uncomfortable because she could feel that she was off-center. Many spiritually gifted people become disoriented as children by their sense of the off-centeredness of the people around them, and their own attempt to adjust themselves to it. However, this same sensitivity to balance can help bring them back to center.

Humility

Shana found the exercise of inhabiting her body very challenging. "This feels awful," she said. "I'm completely stuck in here, stuck to the ground. I feel like I weigh a thousand pounds. Ugh, I feel like I'm a hundred years old." I tried to reassure her that with practice she would feel lighter than she ever had, but she wasn't buying it. She called me after our third session to tell me she wasn't coming back. "It's just not right for me," she said.

About a year later, she called again. She wanted to give it another try. When we met for our first session, she seemed a little sadder than she had the year before. She didn't speak of the events that had occurred since we'd last met, but it seemed like something had humbled her, caused her to take stock of herself, and she felt more accessible. I have often noticed that the people who are most easily able to change and grow have two attributes in common. They have a deep, although sometimes hidden self-love, which causes them to refuse to continue in their limited, suffering state. At the same time, they have humility; they are willing to see themselves as they truly are in the moment, no matter how sad or small or afraid that is.

Now, as we went through the embodiment exercise, Shana seemed more accepting of whatever she felt in each part of her body. When we got to the end of the exercise, I asked her how it had felt. "Not too bad," she answered. "It's kind of sweet in there. I'm kind of a sweet old broad."

"Yes, you are," I said.

Moving as the Quality of Self

I taught Shana how to remain in her body, attuned to the quality of self as she moved. As I explained in chapter 2, even if we attune to the quality of self in just one part of our body, such as our arms, we can feel this quality throughout our whole body. This means that to move through the quality of self, even with just our arms, engages the whole body in the movement. This is very different than my dance training, in which I was taught to "support" the movement of my limbs by holding the rest of my body rigidly still.

I asked Shana to stand and to feel that she inhabited her whole body. Shana now found that she could do this easily. Then I said, "Move your arms slowly out in front of you. Feel that you are inside your arms as you move them. The internal space of your arms is moving through the space of the room.

"Now, with your arms straight out in front of you, attune to the quality of your self inside your arms."

As Shana did this, her whole body lit up with her presence.

I continued, "Staying in your arms, and attuned to the quality of self, slowly open your arms out to the side, perpendicular to your body."

This required some concentration, but Shana found that she could do it. As she moved through the internal space of her arms, she also looked out through the centers of her eyes. We looked right at each other, with instant mutual recognition and contact. As part of this contact, love flowed between us spontaneously. In reaction, Shana quickly projected herself forward into my body, which stopped the flow of love between our two bodies. Then, just as quickly, she reinstated herself within her own body. "Wow, that was interesting," she said. "I can feel you better when I'm in myself."

The Empathic Space

Shana told me that when she did her psychic readings, she had the sense that she was entering into the other person. She realized that one reason she seemed to be resisting developing her practice as a psychic was that each reading left her feeling drained and disoriented. "I seem to become whoever they are," she said. "It can take me until the next day to feel like myself again."

As we continued to practice the Realization Process exercises, Shana became adept at attuning to the space pervading both of us without leaving her own body. She reported that she was starting to bring this same attunement into her psychic readings. "It feels like the space itself is revealing the images now. I don't have to move at all. I just receive whatever is there. In a way, it feels more subtle than the way I used to do readings. And it definitely takes much less effort."

Psychotherapists and bodyworkers have described feeling this same ease in their healing roles as they open to this subtle dimension of their consciousness. Instead of making an effort to be empathic and to say the right thing at the right time, it feels like the healing process unfolds spontaneously. They can receive both the client's communication and their own responses to it in the open space. The uncontrived openness to the moment is now an accepted aspect of therapeutic technique even in fairly conservative quarters of the psychotherapeutic field. Inhabiting the body and attuning to fundamental consciousnesss can facilitate this open-minded, open-hearted approach to the healing encounter.

Disentangling from Our Early Relationships

One day, as Shana and I were practicing the attunement to fundamental consciousness, Shana had a vivid image of her relationship with her mother.

"I can see the two of us sitting together. She was so hard to relate with, I don't know why. But I remember trying to read her, to feel what she was feeling." Then an expression of extreme regret transformed Shana's face. "She passed away three years ago. I'm the only one in the family who didn't get along with her. My two sisters were both so close with her. I don't know what kept me from really loving her." She paused and looked at me guiltily. "I never admitted that to anyone before. I didn't really feel loved by her either, but I think that was just my own fault, I couldn't take in her love. It was one of the things that made me feel so weird in the family. There was this whole circle of love, and I was on the outside of it."

I taught Shana the exercise of imagining her mother in front of her, in order to help her understand how this relationship affected her. I placed an empty chair in front of her, turning my own chair so that I was facing the same direction as she was, a short distance from her. We both looked at the empty chair.

"Begin by feeling that you are inside your whole body at once," I said to her. "Attune to the quality of your self in your whole body.

"Now imagine your mother sitting in the chair in front of you. Feel that the space that pervades your body also pervades her. Let yourself observe whatever occurs in your body as you do this."

As Shana followed these instructions, I felt her heart constrict.

"It's so strange," she said. "There is all this energy coming toward me, but it just doesn't feel like love to me. And her eyes! I can't look at them." Shana turned away from the chair and closed her own eyes tightly, as if to ward off a terrible sight.

"What are her eyes like?" I asked.

With great effort, Shana opened her eyes and glanced back at the image of her mother in the chair. "They're all blurry. It's like she's not looking at me. I don't know why that bothers me so much. Did I just want attention?"

"All children want attention," I said. "And real connection. When we're young, we need to be known in order to know ourselves."

"That's it. She always said how much she loved me, but she didn't know me. What good is it? I know this sounds selfish; the whole family says how selfish I am."

Shana still held her hand, like a shield, over her chest.

I asked, "What's the energy like that's coming out of her chest?"

Shana sat for a long time before answering. "There is love there; there is a sweetness to it," she said, finally. "There's also a lot of need in it. It's like she needs me to give her something that I'm not giving her, and she's angry and hurt. You know, she seems very young. I've never seen this before, but she seems like a little girl."

Shana removed her hand from her chest and relaxed her heart. "I'm very sorry," she whispered to the image of her mother. "I'm very sorry I couldn't take care of you." Shana sat and cried for a long time and her tears seemed to come from a much deeper place than I'd ever seen in her before. I could hear her real voice in her sobs.

She turned to me and became quiet and thoughtful. "I had to protect myself, didn't I? My sisters just merged together with her, they made like a big puddle of love and need. Now they're completely lost." She smiled at me. "I know, I've been pretty lost myself. But they're really nowhere; I go to see them, and it's like there's really no one there. Like they're just going through the motions. But they don't seem to miss themselves, somehow. At least I've known that something was missing."

"Yes," I said. "And even when you were young, you knew there was something to protect."

"I think I'm getting it back now," she said with some wonder in her voice. "I can feel my mind working, my feelings. I feel like I'm really here."

It has often been said that opening to our spiritual essence gives us a sense of being alive to the present moment, of being here, now. When we inhabit our bodies, we have this sense of the present moment throughout our whole being. Recently a man training to be a Realization Process teacher told me that he had spent years attuning to the "now" but he had never before felt the "here."

Spiritual Uses of the Imagination

Shana used her rich imagination to create a persona that both expressed and protected her from the extreme sense of difference and disconnection that she felt in her childhood home. This image of herself as a superior, unearthly being allowed her to hold herself together and preserve enough self-esteem to function in her life. It also maintained her sense of oddness and disconnection from other people, and even obscured the spiritual ground of her being.

However, as Shana became free of her persona, she did not lose her exceptional imagination. She found, instead, that she could consciously use her imagination to help her create the life she wanted. For several months, she spent twenty minutes a day visualizing herself as a psychic reader with a large flourishing practice. In her visualization, she was confident and appreciated by the people who came to work with her. She told me that after just a few weeks of this visualization, her practice had doubled in size.

Although I cannot say how this works, many people have reported this same ability to affect their circumstances or their physical health through the use of their imagination. Tibetan Buddhists have a visualization technique in which they imagine themselves as a deity. This deity visualization can cultivate positive qualities such as compassion or mental clarity. By imagining ourselves as perfect beings, made of light, we may also be able to let go of some of the protective holding patterns that cover up our light. Any image that we use to help better ourselves, however, should be dissolved at the end of the visualization session, or it will itself become a holding pattern.

Embodying ourselves can help us shift from a fantasized life to an authentic experience of ourselves and the world. Spiritual maturity is, above all else, a process of becoming real. To be real means that we are responsive to life in every aspect of our being, that we are fully alive within our bodies.

EXERCISE 13 Feeling How We Have Organized Ourselves in Relation to our Parents

Feel that you are inside your whole body. Find the space outside of your body. Experience that the space inside and outside of your body is the same, continuous space. Picture one of your parents in front of you.

Experience that the space that pervades you also pervades your parent.

Bring your attention to the space pervading your whole body and your parent's head. Allow yourself to see or feel the quality inside their head. Notice any response (such as constriction) in your own body as you do this.

Bring your attention to the space pervading your whole body and your parent's neck. Allow yourself to see or feel the quality inside their neck. Notice any response in your own body as you do this.

Bring your attention to the space pervading your whole body and your parent's chest. Allow yourself to see or feel the quality inside their chest. Notice any response in your own body as you do this.

Bring your attention to the space pervading your whole body and your parent's midsection. Allow yourself to see or feel the quality inside their midsection. Notice any response in your own body as you do this.

Bring your attention to the space pervading your whole body and your parent's pelvis. Allow yourself to see or feel the quality inside their pelvis. Notice any response in your own body as you do this.

If any area of your body constricted during this exercise, go back to the part of your parent's body that evoked this constriction in you. Let yourself feel why you are constricting yourself in relation to your parent.

Now see if you can inhabit the part of your body that you constricted, as you continue to picture your parent in front of you. Attune to the quality of your being associated with that part of your body (understanding, voice, love, power, gender).

Dissolve the image of your parent. Feel that you are inside your whole body, and make deep internal contact with yourself. Attune to the quality of your self in your whole body.

Chapter 8

The Stranger: The Challenge of Acceptance

MANY SPIRITUALLY GIFTED individuals grow up with the sense that they are in exile, that they are "strangers in a strange land." Like visitors in a foreign country, they seem to witness life from a vantage point that native inhabitants do not possess. They see as if from a distance, noticing patterns and disjunctions that cannot be seen up close. They have a talent for seeing situations as a whole, and for seeing beyond the conventional, shared perceptions of their family or their society. Their ability to grasp situations as wholes enables them to find underlying meanings in events that others may not consider.

This sensitivity can develop into visionary insight, an integral aspect of spiritual maturity. It can provide the great pleasure of original, spontaneous thought. It can ripen into wisdom and, when integrated with a developed emotional capacity, can become compassion, the mix of understanding and unconditional love.

This gift can also be a source of loneliness and confusion. As children, these far-sighted individuals often see what they are not supposed to see. They see through the masks of propriety, the forced smiles, or the small and large lies that maintain a veneer of peace in the family home. They are liable to disturb this artificial harmony with their observations, and to be blamed for the discord that results. As the messengers of bad news, they may become the scapegoats for the family's problems. They are the ones who cannot just get along, cannot love nicely like the other family members.

The inability to fit in with one's family is a terrible dilemma for children, who naturally love and need to be loved by the people around them. To have to choose between the truth of their perceptions and the family's affection is an overwhelming challenge. It will significantly affect their beliefs and personality. They may decide that their own perceptions are skewed, and grow up doubting themselves but also distrusting others, not knowing whose account of events to believe. Or they may protect their sensitivity to truth at the cost of depriving themselves of the family warmth, identifying with the role of the unfeeling spectator. They may think of themselves as somehow dangerous, or as pariahs, cast out from the family and societal circle.

As they grow up, their search for something true and meaningful may reveal to them a lack of meaning. They may be acutely aware of the vanity of people's aspirations, or of the mortality that mocks all human ambition. They may be unable to find a direction in their lives that seems worthy of pursuit.

These gifted seers may regard the world as not quite real, as a game or a movie. The desires and losses that seem so important to the players can seem like so much drama, so much ado about nothing, to these sharp observers. They are not participants, and cannot feel truly moved or involved. However, they sometimes remain stuck between the rejection of conventional values and finding or truly honoring their own. Having shunned the accumulation of accomplishments, commitments, and possessions that other people enjoy, they have not yet found their own source of happiness. They live in the limbo between the superficial life that they have rejected and the depths where the reality they seek resides.

Living in a Damaged World

Ben came to work with me because, at fifty, he had still not found a satisfying way to make a living. Having seen himself as a rebel, "living on the edge" all of his life, he was surprised, in his middle years, to feel, deep down, a sense of personal failure. It took almost all of our first session for him to list the different jobs, in many different parts of the United States and Europe, that he had tried since his adolescence.

He related this to me in an off-hand, diffident manner. He seemed to assume that I would see him as a loser, and referred to himself comically as "this schlemiel." He did have one hope for his future. He hoped that the "system" of society would fail. There had been many prophesies that this failure was soon to come. These predictions envisioned a world in chaos, in which banks, computers, and government agencies would be defunct. Ben was eager for the end of a social system that he saw as corrupt, greedy, shallow, and violent. His anticipation did not stop there. He imagined that in the disorder that would ensue, he would finally find his rightful place; he would finally feel motivated to participate.

Apocalyptic visions, in which the wicked are brought to justice and the good are rewarded, have been part of our spiritual legacy at least since the time of the Old Testament prophets. The Bible preserves vivid descriptions of the horror and fury that the prophets felt as they regarded the flawed world around them. Many of the people I work with express this same outrage at the injustice and pollution in the world. Several believe firmly that our society is about to crumble and disappear. They speak of this with either terror or relief, but rarely with sadness. They feel little identity or connection with the society they grew up in, and they would be glad to see it go.

Ben, it turned out, grew up in his own Babylon—within a family of high-powered but untrustworthy people whose values Ben rejected by the time he was five. "I could see the lies on their faces," he told me, "but no one else could. Everyone thought that our family was great."

Yet, because they were his family, he also loved them, and could never entirely extricate himself from their point of view, their "system." Although he left home as soon as he was old enough, and carefully avoided having any sort of financial or social success that would echo his family's ambitions, he also saw himself with their disapproving eyes. This chronic disapproval drained his strength and thwarted his initiative to do anything. He was the outcast, the failure. He was trapped in mid-rebellion, refusing the family's values, but unable to succeed within his own.

Ben knew that he was spiritually gifted. In fact several spiritual masters had encouraged him to develop this gift. He was puzzled that he also kept himself from pursuing this, an achievement so utterly different than anything that anyone in his family had ever attempted. Spiritual practice was a very private endeavor. It would not bring him out into the world that he had rejected; it might even help him to detach from it. When we pondered this question, Ben's eyes filled with longing, but it did not seem like spiritual longing. It was the same expression that he had when he talked about his estrangement from his family. He could not bring himself to leave them behind, to fully become the person that they would never understand. He held onto the hope that his family would change. His clear vision had not just revealed their destructive greed, but also the painfully constrained love beneath their fear and hatred. He wanted the whole system in which they seemed to blindly flourish to be destroyed, so that they could all be free.

At first glance, Ben seemed to be mired in futility. In fact, he was extremely idealistic. Whereas most people filter out the cruel expressions of society, Ben found them intolerable. He believed that life could be different. He imagined that the goodness of human nature would break out of its imprisonment and create a new world on the ruins of the old. In this new world, he would finally be able to really breathe. He would feel invigorated and purposeful.

Ben's body seemed to reflect the passivity and helplessness that he expressed regarding his place in the world. During our sessions, he usually sat with his chest deflated, sunk back into the couch in an attitude of defeat. When I taught him the exercise of inhabiting his body, I noticed that just beneath this deflated exterior was a tautness, like a readiness to defend himself from physical attack. Although he appeared to be in a passive state, he was not actually receptive to his surroundings; he was not letting life in, or out.

When I mentioned to him that I felt he was geared for battle, he assured me that he had never been hit by his family members and that he had always avoided the rough play of his peers. As he became aware of the tautness in his body, however, he remembered that he often did feel a sense of threat in his childhood home. "It was the sounds more than anything else," he said. "The sounds of their voices. My brother and sister were always so loud. They weren't fighting exactly. They were just jockeying for attention, I think. They were so competitive with each other."

"Why didn't you compete with them?" I asked.

His answer to that was just a soft smile, and suddenly I saw the child he had been: an extremely gentle, intelligent, ancient-looking child. Gentleness had not been one of the values of his ambitious family. In his family, only a schlemiel would be gentle.

As Ben practiced inhabiting his body, I also instructed him to feel the softness and tenderness within each part of himself. Because love is one of the essential qualities of our being, we can feel that our whole body is made of love. I also asked him to take a moment, in each part of his body, to value the tenderness that he felt there. Ben seemed both embarrassed and relieved to practice this self-valuing exercise. It was like admitting to something that he had kept secret all of his life.

After several months of practice, we both noticed that the tautness in his forehead had become more pronounced as he had allowed the rest of his body to soften. I asked him to try to enter into this part of himself and see what he felt. As Ben inhabited his forehead, the familiar tautness returned to his body. After a moment, he looked at me with a strange mixture of triumph and guilt.

"Wow," he said, "I never saw this before. I think they're afraid of me. They know that I can see through them and they're afraid. I always thought they rejected me because I just couldn't keep up with them. But they're afraid. Hah! I feel like I have a spike coming out of my forehead."

Ben turned his head slowly from side to side as if to demonstrate the ferocity of this spike. "That does look pretty intimidating," I said.

Having accepted his softness, Ben now had to acknowledge the power of his vision. Both of these attributes had made him an outcast in his childhood home.

In the next few sessions, Ben continued to practice inhabiting his body. He found it most difficult to embody his whole brain. I put a hand on either side of his head and asked him to feel that he was between my hands. This helped him come back into an area of himself that was unfamiliar to him. Like many people, Ben resided mostly in the front of his brain. This was particularly accentuated for Ben who had, since childhood, used his intelligence as a weapon to counter and protect himself from the ignorance around him.

At first he was afraid that it would feel too vulnerable to live within his whole head rather than in the front of it. He could also feel that extending himself out in front of his forehead—his "spike"—displaced him upward and forward, out of his body. When he was finally able to inhabit his whole brain, he was also able to come down into his whole body. Then, for the first time, he could feel the actual quality of power within his midsection. He laughed when he felt that. "I thought you were making that up," he said.

Now I asked him to stand and feel that he was in his whole body at once.

"Attune to the quality of self in your whole body," I said.

As Ben did this, he radiated a strength that I had never seen in him before. At the same time, he exuded the true gentleness and humility that had caused him to feel so isolated during his childhood. Fundamental consciousness, pervading our body, is the integration of yin and yang. It is both potent and gentle, active and receptive, empty and radiant, at the same time.

The acceptance of himself, of both his gentleness and his power, gradually shifted Ben's relationship with the world around him. He still did not like much of what he saw, and he still believed that only an enormous cataclysm could set things right, but he also realized that he did not have to wait for this upheaval in order to live the life he wanted.

Accepting Our Own Wounds

Spiritually sensitive people often feel contaminated by the destructive elements in their environment, and may dedicate themselves to rigorous spiritual practices in order to cleanse themselves of these pollutants and transcend the limitations of worldly life. This approach may also hold them in an adversarial role with their environment and even with their own humanness. It may isolate them in a bubble of attempted perfection that is constantly threatened by their interactions with other people. It may also engender ongoing self-criticism and disappointment as their attempt to purify their thoughts and actions fails. Human beings have tremendous potential for transformation. We can cultivate compassion and gradually empty our minds of destructive thoughts and limiting beliefs, but we cannot truly release the fear and anger from our mind and body if we still feel aversion to the world around us, or if we feel loathing for our own imperfection.

When Ruth came to work with me, although just in her early thirties, she already had an impressive background of spiritual practice. She had studied with highly revered Buddhist and Hindu teachers. She told me that she spent at least two hours a day engaged in spiritual practices. Although I felt a restless energy beneath the surface of her body, she held herself almost completely still, and her eyes held a practiced emptiness, as if there were truly no one there. I was quite familiar with one of the spiritual teachers she mentioned, a feisty old man with a sharp gaze and radiant smile, very different from the vacuous expression of this young woman. I wondered about this discrepancy, about what had gotten lost in translation between teacher and student.

Ruth was surprised and disappointed when I asked her about her childhood. "There is only the present," she told me.

"Yes," I said, "but what we can receive of the present is conditioned and limited by our past."

After what seemed like a moment of internal debate, she submitted to my inquiry. "Well, as it happens, I grew up in a kind of war zone. My parents fought with each other nonstop, like missiles whizzing overhead. When I was nine, I started counting the years that I had to stay there and I left the second I could."

Ruth put herself on a vegan diet when she was sixteen. At seventeen, she left home and joined a spiritual community. They taught her a Sanskrit mantra that she would repeat to herself all day. "I finally got my parents' angry voices out of my head," she said. As Ruth related this to me, I felt admiration for the powerful determination that had compelled her spiritual discipline, and sympathy for the vigorous nature that she was managing to contain within the granite-like statue sitting on my couch.

During her years of practice, Ruth read vast amounts of both Western philosophy and Eastern spiritual literature. She had understood from the Eastern teachings that she did not exist, and that the world was nothing but "a soap bubble." She felt great relief in this. "Insults just roll right off my back now," she said.

"Who is insulting you?" I asked.

"Lots of people insult me!" she said, exasperated at my density. "Insults, bad looks, stupid comments on my diet, any sort of negative remark—the point is that I don't react at all anymore."

"What does it feel like not to exist?" I asked.

"What does it feel like? It doesn't feel like anything. It's not an experience. I'm just no longer here," she answered.

"And what is it like to be no longer here?"

"It's like I am nothing, like anti-matter. I don't even want to say 'I' because there is no 'I,' just emptiness. Not even emptiness because that sounds like a something, *an emptiness*. This is nothing at all."

"So you're not experiencing anything?"

"No. Nothing. I told you, there's no one here to experience anything."

She looked at me defiantly; I was not as approving of her accomplishment as she had expected me to be. Now I understood the mask of emptiness in her eyes and the rigid stillness of her body. She was being nothingness, just as she had read in her books. By continually reminding herself that she did not exist, and that the world around her did not exist, she was able to pass through the many abrasive moments of her days without reacting to them.

However, this abstract understanding of emptiness, or nothingness, is very different than the actual realization of oneself and the world as fundamental consciousness. This transparency does feel like we have become nothing, like we have dissolved into space. But the great mystery is that we are still here, even more present to life than before. We may not, in the moment, be observing or reflecting on ourselves as a separate perceiving, responding being, but we are still here, experiencing, perceiving, responding, even more vividly than before this realization. We do not have to hold ourselves still. We do not have to maintain a perspective of emptiness. We are made of empty stillness. Within this empty ground, life moves fluidly, vividly, and spontaneously.

Ruth felt that she had found the ultimate purification. After years of starving her physical body, she had found a way to rid herself even of herself, but it was not quite working. She still did not feel the peace that she had craved since childhood.

Toward the end of our first session, it became clear why she had sought me out. She had gone to India the year before, planning to spend the rest of her life at the ashram of an Indian teacher. After only a few months, the teacher had shocked her by instructing her to return home. Since then, she had found it difficult to maintain her spiritual practice. She oscillated between feeling anger at what felt like her teacher's rejection of her, and paralyzing doubt about her spiritual abilities, even about the validity of the spiritual path itself.

"Maybe I should drop it all and become a school teacher or maybe an accountant, like my father," she said bitterly. She looked at me with withering disdain. "I thought you would be able to tell me what to do," she said. "But you're just an ordinary person." Then, suddenly helpless, she added, "I need some guidance here, you know."

We sat together in silence for several minutes. Her eyes had lost their fixed emptiness, and now she looked at me with undisguised distrust and anger. Every few moments she shifted her posture slightly with an agitated movement, as if small explosions were erupting within her motionless exterior. I remembered that we were in a "war zone."

Finally I said, "I think that if you try to get rid of yourself, you make a rift in yourself that keeps you from realizing wholeness. And wholeness is naturally empty, naturally disentangled from the flow of life."

Ruth's gaze sharpened. Here was more philosophy; something more for her to understand. "And then, when you get to wholeness, don't you get rid of yourself?" she asked.

"Not really," I said. "It's more like a fruition of your personal self. The self doesn't go away—it awakens. Fundamental consciousness is our own subjectivity experiencing, or realizing, itself. The Zen philosopher Nishitani describes it as the 'absolute near side of ourselves.'[1]

"False constructions of ourselves do fall away as we uncover our essence; we let go of our fixed ideas of ourselves and the world, but the various attributes of our personal self in no way conflict with our realization. Our preferences, aspirations, and particular talents are actually more accessible to us as we uncover the essence of our being."

Ruth absorbed this new information and sat digesting it for a long time. It was as if she had disappeared into the cavernous recesses of her brain, and after a while, I wondered if she would return. Finally I asked, "What do you think of that?"

"Oh," she said. "I'm just wondering if what you said is true." Now fear seemed to mix with the defiance in her expression.

"Yes, that's a good question," I said. "I'm just telling you what I have understood from my experience. You will have your own understanding from your own experience." Ruth looked at me with some surprise, and then a surge of anguish coursed through her body, causing her to fight back tears.

Several months later, when Ruth and I had grown to trust each other, she explained to me why that moment in our dialogue had been important to her. She had suddenly remembered that as a child, she had always understood what each of her parents needed from the other; what they were each fighting for; and how they could find peace with each other. It seemed so clear to her, but when she tried to explain this to each of them, they dismissed her insights as if they were nonsense. Her father's favorite retort was, "You don't know anything."

"I think that phrase is echoing in all of my cells," she said. "I've tried really hard to know something."

As I taught Ruth the exercise of inhabiting her body, the agitation in her body became more obvious. She shifted her position frequently, and shook her hands or tossed her head, as if trying to rid herself of a buzzing mosquito. Finally, she almost shouted at me, "I don't want to do this. I don't want to be here. I don't have to be here."

As those words reverberated in the room, I decided to be silent. She didn't need me to give her permission to leave. And her words had a deeper meaning, a meaning that had shaped her life, without ever being fully stated.

In the silence, Ruth began to settle more deeply within her body, and the shaking and tossing stopped. Finally she said, "It feels like humility."

"To be here?"

"Yes. It's like I have to accept this moment, to actually live it. To just be space like this feels very humble."

"Does it feel vulnerable?" I asked.

Ruth sat with that question for a moment. Then she smiled, and suddenly her whole body seemed to come to life. "No," she said. "It feels very strong. Humble and strong."

As we continued, I focused the instructions for the exercise on helping her settle within her body. "Feel that you are inside your legs. Let yourself settle within your legs. Feel that you are inside your pelvis. Let yourself settle within your pelvis."

With some practice, Ruth could feel how she could rest within each part of her body. She also felt how each part of the internal space of her body rested on the part below it, such as the internal space of the chest resting on the internal space of her midsection. This helped her to feel the internal continuity of herself, as if she were a continuous column of internal space. In the same way, each quality of her being rested on the quality beneath it (such as the quality of love resting on the quality of power), so that all of the qualities were continuous with each other. Together, they produced a single quality, a felt sense of her aliveness.

When Ruth could clearly feel that the space inside and outside of her body was the same continuous space, I continued with the instructions.

"Let yourself feel that there is no difference between your self and the space," I said. "You are the space." Ruth was now able to do this easily. She had disappeared, and yet she was still there, alert and grinning at me.

I continued, "Now, as that space, you can let go of all of the content of experience. You can let go of your inner experience and let go of the room. Everything will still be there; you are just letting go of your grasp on it."

Ruth said, "I can feel myself not wanting to do that."

"Why is that?" I asked.

"I think that if I let go, those missiles will start up again. Some catastrophe will happen." Then she looked at me with some of her old defiance. "You're going to tell me that everything happens for a reason," she said. "Just let it unfold; everything happens perfectly."

I met her gaze silently. Ruth continued, "But I can't know that, can I? I'm done just believing things."

We sat together in the silence for another moment. Then Ruth seemed to relax. "I think that I have to accept reality, even if it is bad, even if something doesn't have a 'good reason' for happening. I need to let life keep flowing, good and bad. I can do that." A deep sense of contentment entered the space. She was on her way to making peace with the rough, unpredictable world, not by ignoring it, but by encompassing it.

The acceptance of our humanness is a necessary requirement for uncovering the transcendent ground of our humanness. If we use our intelligence to separate ourselves from our emotions and sensations, or from the world around us, then we fragment ourselves and obscure the unified essence of our being.

Wherever we are in contact with the internal space of our body, we are open to life. And when we are open to life, we also transcend life. We both experience and disentangle from our experience at the same time. Life flows through us.

EXERCISE 14 Walking as Fundamental Consciousness

I suggest that you practice this exercise outside, feeling that the space that pervades your body also pervades the sky, earth, trees, and other forms in nature. Find a stretch of even ground, where you can walk comfortably.

Stand with your eyes open. Feel that you are inside your feet. Experience that there is no separation between you and the ground. Feel that you are inside your whole body at once. Attune to the quality of your self inside your whole body.

Walk slowly, staying inside your whole body and attuned to the quality of self.

Now find the space outside your body. Experience that the space inside and outside your body is the same, continuous space.

Walk slowly, experiencing space pervading your whole body and the environment at the same time. Stay inside your body as you do this.

• • •

So much of our religious legacy, in both the East and West, devalues life. This is not a mature teaching. To reveal the actual spiritual dimension of life, we need to allow our experience to register with its full impact, throughout our whole body and being. By inhabiting our body, we can both tolerate this impact and cultivate its depth. We become the unbreakable transparency and the spontaneous responsiveness of our fundamental nature.

Recently the young man that I mentioned in the introduction told me that since coming into his body, he feels "less gap" between himself and the world. A sense of being more present in his body and looking out at his surroundings has begun to replace his life-long struggle with self-consciousness, his paralyzing fear of being seen and judged by other people.

When he said this to me, I suddenly remembered standing on a subway platform many years ago and feeling so different from other people that I thought I would never be able to bridge the gulf between myself and the world around me. Since then, the gradual ripening inward, the filling up of my body as fundamental consciousness, as the pure subjectivity that is the same in all of us, has erased this illusion of distance between myself and other people.

I hope that this book has helped you feel more accepting and appreciative of your sensitivity, your emotional depth, and your big mind. Each of these gifts is an entranceway into your true nature, which is more miraculous than anything we can imagine. As we have seen in the people I have described here, and as you may know from your own experience, these gifts may produce pain as well as joy. They call on us to heal specific wounds, to meet specific challenges in our relationship with the world. They create, for each of us, our unique path to the vast expanse at the core of our being. We know that we belong here when we find within our own body the one ground that connects us intimately and directly with all life.

Notes

CHAPTER 1 Embodiment

1. Keiji Nishitani, *Religion and Nothingness* (Berkeley and Los Angeles: University of California Press, 1982), 164.

2. Heinz R. Pagels, *The Cosmic Code* (New York: Bantam Books, 1983).

3. John Daido Loori, dharma talk given at Zen Mountain Monastery, circa 1982.

CHAPTER 2 The Realization Process

1. John Briggs, *Fractals: The Patterns of Chaos* (New York: Touchstone, 1992).

CHAPTER 3 Healing from Relational Trauma

1. Joseph LeDoux, *The Emotional Brain* (New York: Touchstone, 1996).

2. Elizabeth F. Howell, *The Dissociative Mind* (New York: Routledge, 2005).

3. Ibid.

CHAPTER 4 **Thin Skin**

1. Elaine N. Aron, *The Highly Sensitive Person* (New York: Broadway Books, 1997).

2. Carol Kranowitz, *The Out-of-Sync Child: Recognizing and Coping with Sensory Processing Disorder* (New York: Perigee Trade, 2006).

CHAPTER 7 **Shape Shifters**

1. Carlos Castaneda, *The Teaching of Don Juan: A Yaqui Way of Knowledge* (Berkeley: University of California Press, 1968).

CHAPTER 8 **The Stranger**

1. Nishitani, *Religion and Nothingness,* 106.

About the Author

JUDITH BLACKSTONE, PHD, developed the Realization Process, an innovative integration of nondual spiritual awakening, psychological healing, and embodiment. She offers workshops and teacher trainings in the Realization Process throughout the United States and Europe. She is a psychotherapist in New York City and author of *The Intimate Life*, *The Empathic Ground*, *The Enlightenment Process*, and *The Subtle Self*. She is the founding director of the Nonduality Institute in New York City.

Judith began performing at age ten with a modern dance company in New York City. She danced for fifteen years until a back injury brought her to the spiritual path. She has been a meditation practitioner for almost four decades, studying with Hindu, Zen, and Tibetan Buddhist teachers. The Realization Process emerged outside of traditional lineages, in response to the needs of contemporary seekers. For more information on the Realization Process, visit judithblackstone.com.

About Sounds True

SOUNDS TRUE IS a multimedia publisher whose mission is to inspire and support personal transformation and spiritual awakening. Founded in 1985 and located in Boulder, Colorado, we work with many of the leading spiritual teachers, thinkers, healers, and visionary artists of our time. We strive with every title to preserve the essential "living wisdom" of the author or artist. It is our goal to create products that not only provide information to a reader or listener, but that also embody the quality of a wisdom transmission.

For those seeking genuine transformation, Sounds True is your trusted partner. At SoundsTrue.com you will find a wealth of free resources to support your journey, including exclusive weekly audio interviews, free downloads, interactive learning tools, and other special savings on all our titles.

To listen to a podcast interview with Sounds True publisher Tami Simon and author Judith Blackstone, please visit SoundsTrue.com/bonus/BelongingHere.

sounds true
WAKING UP THE WORLD